THE AMERICAN VIGNOLA

A Guide to the Making of Classical Architecture

WILLIAM R. WARE

With Introductory Notes by

JOHN BARRINGTON BAYLEY *and* HENRY HOPE REED

and a New Foreword by

ARTHUR ROSS

DOVER PUBLICATIONS
Garden City, New York

Bibliographical Note

This Dover edition, first published in 1994, is an unabridged republication of the edition first published by W. W. Norton & Company, Inc., New York, in 1977 (original edition, 1903). The present edition is published by special arrangement with Classical America, New York. A new foreword has been specially prepared for this republication, and the list of Classical America publications has been updated.

Library of Congress Cataloging-in-Publication Data

Ware, William R. (William Robert), 1832–1915.
 The American Vignola : a guide to the making of classical architecture / William R. Ware ; with introductory notes by John Barrington Bayley and Henry Hope Reed and a new foreword by Arthur Ross.
  p.   cm. — (The Classical America series in art and architecture)
 "Republication of the edition first published by W. W. Norton & Company, Inc., New York, in 1977 (original edition, 1903)"—T.p. verso.
 ISBN-13: 978-0-486-28310-4
 ISBN-10: 0-486-28310-0
 1. Architecture—Orders. 2. Architecture, Classical, 3. Architecture—Details. 4. Vignola, 1507–1573. I. Title. II. Series.
NA2815.W3 1994
721—dc20   94-20782
                                                                    CIP

Manufactured in the United States by LSC Communications Book LLC
28310014   2021
www.doverpublications.com

CONTENTS

Part I. Plates I-XVIII

———

Part II. Arches and Vaults, Roofs and Domes, Doors and Windows, Walls and Ceilings, Steps and Staircases

FOREWORD TO
THE DOVER EDITION

by Arthur Ross

IT is indeed rewarding and timely for Classical America, under the guidance of its distinguished President, Henry Hope Reed, to launch a second edition of this reprint, originally issued in 1977, of William R. Ware's *The American Vignola*.

The American Renaissance in architecture, which flourished from 1890 to 1930, featured the classical principles of architecture. Out of fashion for almost two generations, this style may be about to enjoy a new renaissance. The architectural schools of our country will be in need of an appropriate textbook on the classical. It was Giacomo Barozzi da Vignola who first codified the rules of classical architecture for the Italian Renaissance. These teachings were turned into a practical tool by William R. Ware, the outstanding teacher of American architecture at the turn of the century, and his instruction is embodied in *The American Vignola*, first published in 1903.

William R. Ware was a force in the launching of the American Renaissance and the City Beautiful Movement when a professor at Columbia University. During that creative and ebullient era, initiated by the World's Columbian Exposition of 1893 in Chicago, we Americans embellished our cities, towns and campuses with unparalleled grandeur from the Atlantic to the Pacific, from the Canadian to the Mexican border.

This reprint of *The American Vignola* as a textbook for architectural use expresses Classical America's confidence in a rebirth of the teaching and artistic disciplines of Vignola as recast for our use by William R. Ware.

INTRODUCTORY NOTES
for the Classical America Edition

by John Barrington Bayley and Henry Hope Reed

THIS book is the last living (in print) descendant of those studies which saw the recovery of the lost laws of classical architecture: studies which began with Bramante and Raphael when the ruins of ancient Rome—then so much more extensive than today—were explored and sketched and measured. Giacomo Barozzi da Vignola codified the rules of classical architecture for the Italian Renaissance.

As you will see from the Preface, William R. Ware's *American Vignola* started on West Tenth Street in Richard Morris Hunt's studio, where the practice of classical architecture was being rediscovered and where the American Renaissance began. Ware codified Vignola for the American Renaissance.

Giacomo Barozzi da Vignola (from a contemporary engraving)

Vignola's original book—*Regola delle cinque ordini d'architettura*—had rather broad wood-cuts and generalized information. It was a basis for further developments of architectural feeling by way of the countless sketches in the various media which kept alive at all times a sense of the whole object in three dimensions whether it was a detail or a complete façade. This method guaranteed the clarity and the simplicity which are at the heart of the Grand Manner. The old Italians never made a mistake because they had the great models all around them; our architects and draftsmen did not.

Ware's *Vignola* had engravings and very precise information ideally suited to the sharp pencil of the draftsman against T square and triangle. It was eminently suited to the times. Architecture was no longer a matter of churches, palaces, villas, and squares reared with infinite care over long years.

The American Renaissance built more domes, pediments, colonnades, and classical buildings in general than any other period in history. We built in marble and bronze where Europeans used limestone and wood. We have the greatest obelisk and the greatest colossal statue.

We built capitols, law courts, civic ensembles, and monuments on a scale unknown since antiquity. We built new kinds of buildings: museums, libraries, railroad stations, clubs, hotels, skyscrapers, and stores in which our architects and engineers worked out solutions which were and are the basis for all future developments. We built with unparalleled grandeur, and our architecture led the world.

It is the hope of the directors of Classical America that this book which served the American Renaissance so well may stand to serve a new renaissance.

J. B. B.

William Robert Ware (Courtesy Avery Library, Columbia University)

In his preface to the first volume of this book, William Robert Ware recalled a brief but important moment in his education in architecture. The occasion was early in 1859 in the Studio Building which once stood at 51 West Tenth Street in New York City. Unfamiliar with classical architecture—at the time he knew only Gothic well—he was trying to draw a Doric column based on Vignola's manual of the five orders when his master, Richard Morris Hunt, showed him how to lay out a column in no time. From the lesson was to come, in time, *The American Vignola*.

The place was Hunt's atelier, very much of an innovation on the American architectural scene. Henry Van Brunt, Ware's future partner, who was also there, described the experience. "Those of us who were fortunate enough to be placed under the immediate influence of Hunt as his pupils will never forget either the wealth of his resources or the inspiring nature of his instruction," he wrote. "These resources were placed at our disposal with a most lavish hand . . ."—resources which contrasted sharply with the typical architectural instruction of the day. "The study of architecture at that time was pursued under the most discouraging conditions. The art was ill understood and indeed hardly respected by the public," Van Brunt explained. "There were no schools in which it was recognized as a desirable subject for study. There were but few books available and our traditions were eminently provincial. Examples of good work were so rare that our ideals of perfection were incoherent and doubtful and were swayed, now in one direction and now in another, by the literary warfare then prevailing between Gothic and classic camp . . ."

Ware, as we can see, was present at the start of true architectural training in this country. What is more, he was to have a large part in shaping its development because, not long after, he headed America's first architectural school at the Massachusetts Institute of Technology and, later, Columbia University's School of Architecture.

William Robert Ware was as solid a product of "the home of the bean and the cod" as you could find. He was born in 1832 into a clerical family in Cambridge. His father was a Unitarian minister and a professor at the Harvard Divinity School. His grandfather had been a Congregational minister who had also taught at the Divinity School. The future architect and writer was to go to Phillips Exeter Academy, Harvard College, and the Lawrence Scientific School. After a short stint in a Boston architectural office, he entered the Hunt atelier. Others there at the time, besides Henry Van Brunt, were George Brown Post, who was to design the campus of the College of the City of New York and the New York Stock Exchange, and Frank Furness, architect of the Pennsylvania Academy of Fine Arts and the Fine Arts Building of the University of Pennsylvania.

Not long after, in 1863, he began his partnership with Van Brunt, which was to last formally until 1883. The firm soon had a solid practice in the Boston region, its best-known building being Harvard's splendid Memorial Hall (1874–1878).

Paralleling his practice was his career as a teacher of architecture. In 1865 he was named director of M.I.T.'s School of Architecture and, because it was the country's first, he had to organize it to the last detail. Sixteen years later, he was called to New York to start another, that at Columbia, and there he remained until his retirement in 1903.

What he did at both schools was to adapt to the American condition the methods of the famous École des Beaux Arts in Paris, the same methods he first discovered under Hunt. They consisted of a system of instruction based on the study of the traditional styles, with particular emphasis on the classical. The students learned by executing set projects in competition and by progressing from project to project. The emphasis was on the building's plan in the belief that a good plan inevitably resulted in a handsome building. Architectural drawing was underscored. At Columbia, this last, for example, went as follows over a four-year period: tracing, copying, graphic construction, graphic discussion (the object drawn from different aspects), pen work, brush work, outdoor sketching, and the study of the orders.

Ware's system differed from the Parisian model in that he offered general surveys of the cultures which produced the several styles. For him, the architect had to be a cultivated individual as well as a technician. His interest in this was, of course, made easier by the fact that, in Columbia's case, his school was part of a great liberal arts university, as are most American architectural schools today. And there is no doubt that it was this interest which led to the creation of Columbia's incomparable Avery Library, the nation's finest collection of architectural books.

In addition to teaching, Ware served on architectural commissions and as a consultant. He was a member of the board of the Pan-American Exposition (Buffalo, New York) of 1900. More important was his serving as adviser, together with Frederick Law Olmsted, to the trustees of Columbia University on the design of the Morningside Heights campus. The famous competition was won by Charles Follen McKim.

He also wrote pamphlets, articles, and books. Among the last were *Greek Ornament* (1878), *Modern Perspective* (1883), *The American Vignola* (1902–1906), and *Shades and Shadows* (1912–1913).

Only one of them, *The American Vignola*, continued in print over the years, and then only in an obscure, much abbreviated version. The present edition in the Classical America Series in Art and Architecture is the first complete one in recent years as well as the first to be made available to the general public.

There would appear to be considerable divergence between Ware the architect and Ware the writer. Most of his buildings, done with Van Brunt, were Gothic. Harvard's Memorial Hall, for example, is Gothic in the manner of John Ruskin. When it came to writing, however, he turned to the classical.

Ware's eclecticism was very characteristic of nineteenth-century architecture. Like his master, Hunt, who began with exercises in Viollet-le-Duc Gothic only to shift to the classical, Ware also changed course. The coming of the American Renaissance and the triumph of the Columbian Exposition of 1893 made the shift all but obligatory.* Not surprisingly, it was the exposition's central classical design which influenced McKim's project for the Columbia campus, a domed building surrounded by structures of a lower, uniform height. To what extent Ware as consultant influenced the trustees in their choice is not known, but it is not without significance that the key classical architectural manual of the era came out of a university whose campus was by far the best of those built in the American Renaissance manner.

In entitling his manual *The American Vignola*, Ware was not simply remembering the hours he struggled to draw out a column, he was turning to the Renaissance architect who had produced the handiest method of executing the five orders; this was in Vignola's *Regola delle cinque ordini d'architettura* (1562). It consisted of a modular interpretation, the module being half the diameter of the lower part of the column, Ware's being the full diameter. Vignola was not the first to offer the method, but his book was the first to do so with clarity and a minimum of argument.

In contrast to Ware's manual, with its many illustrations as well as plates and with its overview from the study of moldings to stairs and vaults, Vignola's *Regola* is limited to thirty-two plates. His five orders he found in the remains of ancient Rome, and he specifically mentions that he took the Doric from the theater of Marcellus and the Corinthian from the porch of the Pantheon. His book closes with an entablature of his own invention.

The *Regola* proved very successful. Subsequent editions were enlarged with new plates, most drawn from Vignola's own work, especially the Farnese Palace at Caprarola (Villa Caprarola in the Ware text). By 1700 the book numbered sixteen Italian editions, five French, two German, two English, and two Russian as well as several in Spanish and Dutch. In the eighteenth century, while the English, Germans, and Russians switched their allegiance to Palladio, the French and the Italians remained loyal to Vignola. (Most of the main American Renaissance compositions up to 1915 were in the French or Italian modes.)

In the nineteenth century Vignola was attacked—as was Palladio, for that matter—especially by the "Goths," Viollet-le-Duc and Ruskin. There were those who maintained that his rule book crushed initiative on the part of an aspiring architect. That the book was a beginning, a jumping-off point for the architect with talent, was often forgotten; and those without talent it at least saved from error. In his *Architecture of Humanism*, Geoffrey Scott wrote of "the academic influence," meaning the books of Vitruvius, Serlio, Palladio, and others besides Vignola, that 'it provided a canon of forms by which even the uninspired architect could secure at least a measure of distinction; and genius, where it existed, could be trusted to use this scholastic learning as a means and not an end." It is this canon of forms which Ware has simply made American.

If there was criticism from the likes of Viollet-le-Duc and Ruskin, there were also those who knew all along that only the classical furnished a prevailing standard in architecture—a standard denied other historic styles.

---

*Certain college campuses (notably Yale, Duke, and Princeton universities), suburban churches, and a handful of skyscrapers would after 1900 be built in Gothic styles.

How different in time, place, background, and education were Ware and Vignola! Ware came of a line of clergymen of Protestant New England, where learning was at a premium. Vignola came of a family presumably of craftsmen and was a solid product of Catholic and Renaissance Italy. He was born Giacomo Barozzi in 1507 in the town of Vignola, about twenty miles west of Bologna. He began as an apprentice painter in Bologna, working for Sebastiano Serlio and Baldassare Peruzzi, both of whom were painters before becoming architects. Only after going to Rome in 1530 and working at the Vatican under Peruzzi, Jacopo Melighino, and Antonio da Sangallo the Younger did he shift to architecture. Not long after, he was in the Accademia Vitruviano, where, with Francesco Primaticcio, he assembled a collection of ancient sculpture and executed plaster casts of great statues for Francis I of France. In 1541 he accompanied Primaticcio to Paris and Fontainebleau. Two years later he was in Bologna, where he designed his first building, the Palazzo Bocchi. In 1546 his career took wing on his becoming a retainer of Pier Luigi Farnese, Duke of Parma and Piacenza, and from then on he was a retainer of the great family. When Michelangelo parted company with the Farnese, Vignola took charge of the construction of the Palazzo Farnese in Rome, completing chimney pieces and portals. In 1551, under Pope Paul III (Farnese), he was at work on the Villa Papa Giulo III, a commission he shared with Giorgio Vasari and Bartolommeo Ammanati. Then followed San Andrea in the Via Flaminia, the Orti Farnesiani on the Palatine (which was destroyed when excavations began there in the 1850s), some work on the Papal Chancellery, and his greatest monument, the Palazzo Farnese at Caprarola for Alexander, Cardinal Farnese, grandson of the pope. In the 1560s he was working on St. Peter's and executing the plan and the first design for the façade of the Gesù. He is also credited with the Villa Lante at Bagnaia near Viterbo. In addition to his *Regola*, he wrote a book on perspective published posthumously. He was still in charge of works at St. Peter's when he died in 1573. He lies buried, fittingly enough, in the Pantheon.

H. H. R.

General Editors' Note on This Edition of *The American Vignola*

Part I is based on the fourth edition of 1905 and Part II on the first edition of 1906—both published by the International Textbook Company of Scranton, Pennsylvania. The editors are especially grateful to Adolph K. Placzek of the Avery Library, and to Pierce Rice and Michael George for help in finding copies of the book from which this edition is adapted and, above all, to Arthur Ross, whose grant made the new publication of the book possible.

Detail of the top of the massive table of variegated marble designed by Vignola for Cardinal Alessandro Farnese (The Metropolitan Museum of Art, Harris Brisbane Dick Fund, 1958)

PART I

The Five Orders

PREFACE

IN January, 1859, I went from Mr. Edward Cabot's office in Boston, where I had been for two or three years, to join the little company of half a dozen young men who were studying architecture in the Studio Building in Tenth Street, under the inspiration of Mr. Richard Hunt. Mr. Hunt had just returned from Paris, and was eager to impart to younger men, though we were not much his juniors, what he had learned in the *École des Beaux-Arts* and in work upon the New Louvre. We had all, I believe, had more or less of office experience, but those were the days when the Gothic Revival was at its height, and Mr. Hunt found most of us unfamiliar with Classical details and quite unskilled in their use. I, at any rate, knew hardly a touch of them, and I remember well the day when, as I was carefully drawing out a Doric Capital according to the measurements given in my *Vignola*, Mr. Hunt took the pencil out of my hand and, setting aside the whole apparatus of *Modules* and *Minutes*, showed me how to divide the height of my Capital into thirds, and those into thirds, and those again into thirds, thus getting the sixths, ninths, eighteenths, twenty-sevenths, and fifty-fourths of a Diameter which the rules required, without employing any larger divisor than two or three.

It seemed as if this method, so handy with the Doric Capital, might be applied to other things, and I forthwith set myself to studying the details of all the Orders, and to devising for my own use simple rules for drawing them out. The present work presents the results of these endeavors. Experience in the class room has, meanwhile, amplified and extended them, and they have at many points been improved by the suggestions of my colleagues.

I am particularly indebted to Professor Hamlin and to Mr. W. T. Partridge for some ingenious applications of the 45-degree line to the Doric Entablature and to the Corinthian Capital, and for an analogous employment of the 60-degree line.

Finding that the plates in which, for the convenience of my own students, I have embodied these results are somewhat in demand by others, I now publish them in the present volume, adding such text and marginal illustrations as the subject matter seems to require. The Plates have been drawn out for me anew by Mr. Partridge, as have also most of the Illustrations. The rest have been taken from standard publications, especially from Bühlmann's "*Architecture of Classical Antiquity and the Renaissance*," which has furnished twenty-six of the Figures.

The forms and proportions here set forth are, in the main, those worked out by Giacomo Barozzi da Vignola and first published by him at Rome in the year 1563, as those which, in his judgment, best embodied the best practice of the ancient Romans. Other systems have been presented by Alberti, Palladio, Scamozzi, Serlio, Sir William Chambers, and others. But Vignola's Orders have generally been accepted as the standard. His works have been frequently republished, and recourse must be had to them for minute information in regard to details. But the dimensions given in this book, and the methods of determining them here described, will suffice for the execution of all drawings and designs which are made to a small scale.

This volume is concerned only with Columns, Pilasters and Entablatures, Pediments, Pedestals, and Balustrades. The employment of these Elements in the Composition of Doors and Windows, Wall Surfaces, external and internal, Staircases, Towers, and Spires, Arches and Arcades, Vaults and Domes, and other architectural features, will, I hope, at a later day be made the subject of a separate treatise which will be the natural sequel to this one.

After the chief part of this volume was in press my attention was directed to a somewhat similar work by the celebrated James Gibbs, the architect of St. Martin's-in-the-Fields and of St. Mary-le-Strand. He published in London, in 1732, a series of plates showing the Orders and their applications with a brief descriptive text. The title page reads: "Rules for Drawing the Several Parts of Architecture in a more Exact and Easy Manner than has been heretofore Practiced, by which all Fractions, in dividing the Principal Members and their Parts, are Avoided." The book begins with an *Address to the Reader* which opens as follows:

"Upon examination of the common ways of drawing the Five Orders of Architecture, I thought there might be a method found out so to divide the principal Members and their Parts, both as to their Heights and Projections, as to avoid Fractions. And having tried one Order with success, I proceeded to another, till at length I was satisfied it would answer my intention in all; and I doubt not but that the Method here proposed will be acknowledged by proper Judges to be the most exact, as well as the easiest, that hath as yet been published."

I find on examining the plates that, though they follow an entirely different system, they have anticipated some of the methods of the present work.

WILLIAM R. WARE.

October 1, 1902.
SCHOOL OF ARCHITECTURE, COLUMBIA UNIVERSITY

THE AMERICAN VIGNOLA

The Five Orders

INTRODUCTION

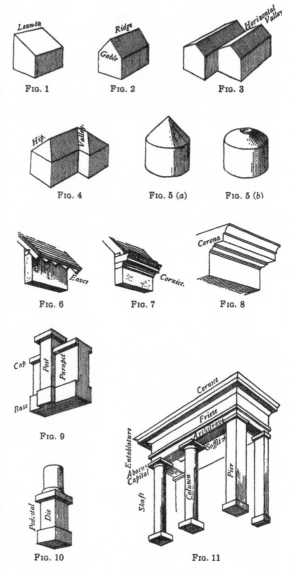

A BUILDING is a shelter from rain, sun, and wind. This implies a *Roof*, and *Walls* to support it. If the walls entirely enclose the space within, there are *Doorways* for access, and *Windows* for light. Roofs and walls, doors and windows are the essential features of buildings.

Roofs may be flat, sloping, or curved. A roof with one slope is called a *Lean-to*, Fig. 1. When two sloping roofs rest upon parallel walls and lean against one another, they meet in a horizontal *Ridge*, Fig. 2, at the top, and form a *Gable* at each end. Roofs that rise from the same wall in opposite directions form a *Horizontal Valley*, Fig. 3, at the wall. If two walls make a projecting angle, their roofs intersect in an inclined line called a *Hip*, Fig. 4. If the walls meet in a reentering angle, the inclined line of intersection is called a *Valley*. Circular walls carry conical, Fig. 5 (*a*) or domical roofs, Fig. 5 (*b*).

If there is more than one story, the flat roof of the lower story becomes the *Floor* of the story above. If the roof extends beyond the wall that supports it, the projection is called the *Eaves*, Fig. 6. If the wall also projects, to support the extension of the roof, the projection is called a *Cornice*, Fig. 7. The principal member of a cornice, which projects like a shelf and crowns the wall, is called a *Corona*, Fig. 8.

Walls are generally made wider just at the bottom, so as to get a better bearing on the ground. This projection is the *Base*, Fig. 9. A similar projection at the top is called a *Cap*, or, if it projects much, a *Cornice*, as has been said. A low wall is called a *Parapet*. A short piece of wall about as long as it is thick is called a *Post*, and if it supports something, a *Pedestal*, Fig. 10, the part between its Cap and Base is then the *Die*. A tall post is called a *Pier*, Fig. 11, if it is square, and a *Column* if it is round. Caps of piers and columns are called *Capitals*, and the part between the Cap and the Base, the *Shaft*. The flat upper member of a Capital is called the *Abacus*.

5

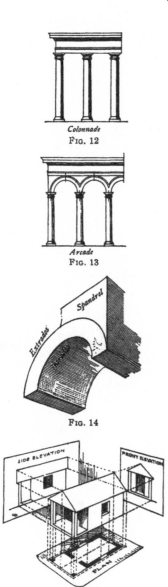

Colonnade
FIG. 12

Arcade
FIG. 13

FIG. 14

FIG. 15

A beam that spans the space between two piers or columns, or between a pier or column and a wall, is called an *Architrave*, or *Epistyle*. Above it, between the Architrave and the Cornice, there is generally a little strip of wall called the *Frieze*. Architrave, Frieze, and Cornice constitute the *Entablature*. A series of columns is called a *Colonnade*, Fig. 12. The spaces between piers or columns are sometimes spanned by *Arches*, a series of which is called an *Arcade*, Fig. 13.

The space between two parallel walls is sometimes covered by a sort of continuous arch, called a *Vault*, instead of by a floor or roof, Fig. 14.

The under surface of a beam or architrave is called its *Soffit*, and the same name is used also for the *Intrados*, or under surface of an arch or vault. The upper surface, or back of an arch, is called the *Extrados*, and the triangular space of wall above is called a *Spandrel*.

The Wall, the Pier, and the Column, with or without a Pedestal, constitute the chief supporting members; the Frieze and Cornice, with the roof that rests upon them, constitute the chief part of the load they carry. The Architrave, the Arches, and the Spandrels form part of the load, relatively to what is below them, but are supporting members relatively to what is above them.

Besides being valuable as a shelter, a building may be in itself a noble and delightful object, and architects are builders who, by giving a building good proportions and fine details, and by employing beautiful materials, make it valuable on its own account, independently of its uses. Their chief instruments in this work are Drawings, both of the whole building and, on a larger scale, of the different features which compose it and of their details, which are often drawn full size. These drawings comprise Plans, Sections, Elevations, and Perspective Views, Fig. 15. They serve to explain the intention of the architects to their clients and to their workmen.

MOLDINGS—PLATE I

The simplest decorative details and those that are most universally used in buildings are called *Moldings*. They are plane or cylindrical surfaces, convex, concave, or of double curvature, and they are sometimes plain and sometimes enriched by carving. They are called by various technical names: Greek, Latin, Italian, French, and English. The cross-section of a molding is called its *Profile*.

A small plane surface is called a *Band*, *Face*, or *Fascia*, Fig. 16, and if very small a *Fillet*, *Raised* or *Sunk*, Fig. 17, *Horizontal*, *Vertical*, or *Inclined*.

A convex molding is called an *Ovolo*, Fig. 18, *Torus*, Fig. 19, or *Three-quarter Molding*, Fig. 20, according to the amount of the curvature of its profile. A small Torus is called a *Bead*, Fig. 21, *Astragal*, or *Reed*, and an elliptical one, a *Thumb Molding*, Fig. 22. Concave moldings are, in like manner, called *Cavetto*, Fig. 23, *Scotia*, Fig. 24, or *Three-quarter Hollow*, but the term Scotia (darkness) is often used for any hollow molding. A Cavetto tangent to a plane surface is called a *Congé*, Fig. 25.

A molding with double curvature is called a *Cyma*, or Wave Molding. If the tangents to the curve at top and bottom are horizontal, as if the profile were cut from a horizontal wavy line, it is called a *Cyma Recta*, Fig. 26; if vertical, as if cut from a vertical line, a *Cyma Reversa*, Fig. 27. The Cyma Recta is sometimes called Cyma Reversa, Fig. 26 (c), when it is turned upside down. But this leads to confusion. The Cymas vary also, Fig. 28, in the shape and relative size of their concave and convex elements. A small Cyma is called a *Cymatium*. A small molding placed above a Band, or any larger molding, as a decoration, is also called a *Cymatium*, Fig. 29, whatever its shape.

When a convex and a concave molding, instead of being tangent, come together at an angle, they constitute a *Beak Molding*, Fig. 30.

Some architectural features, such as Bases, Caps, and Balusters, consist entirely of moldings. Others consist mainly of plane surfaces, moldings being employed to mark the boundary between different features, as between the Architrave and Frieze, or between different members of the

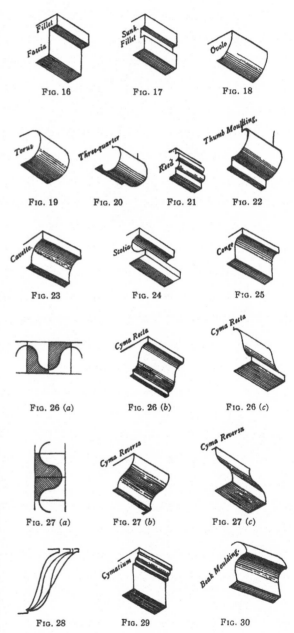

Fig. 16   Fig. 17   Fig. 18

Fig. 19   Fig. 20   Fig. 21   Fig. 22

Fig. 23   Fig. 24   Fig. 25

Fig. 26 (a)   Fig. 26 (b)   Fig. 26 (c)

Fig. 27 (a)   Fig. 27 (b)   Fig. 27 (c)

Fig. 28   Fig. 29   Fig. 30

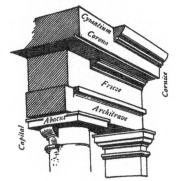

FIG. 31

FIG. 32

FIG 33

same feature, as between the Shaft of a column and its Capital, Fig. 31. In these cases the moldings, since they occur on the edges of the stone blocks, indicate, while they conceal, the position of the joints of the masonry. Moldings are often placed also in the internal angle where two plane surfaces meet, as is the case between the Frieze and the Corona of the Cornice, and under the Abacus of the Capital. When placed upon the external angle formed by two planes, they are, in the Gothic Styles, Fig. 32, often cut in, so as to lie below the surface of both planes, but in the Classical Styles, they project beyond the plane of one of the surfaces, like a little cornice, as is often seen in the Abacus of a Capital.

Horizontal Moldings, separating plane surfaces, are called a *String-Course*, Fig. 33.

TABLE OF MOLDINGS, PLATE I

Plane.—Face, Band, or Fascia; Beveled, Inclined, or Splay Face; Fillet, vertical, horizontal, or beveled, Raised or Sunk.

Convex.—Ovolo, or Quarter Round; Torus, or Half Round; Thumb Molding, or Elliptical Torus; Three-quarter Round; Bead, Astragal, or Reed; Three-quarter Bead.

Concave.—Cavetto or Quarter Hollow; Congé; Half Hollow; Scotia; Three-quarter Hollow.

Double Curvature.—Cyma Recta; Cyma Reversa; Cymatium; Beak Molding.

Besides the differences of size and shape already mentioned, and indicated in the table, moldings of the same name differ in the kind of curve they employ. They may be arcs, either of circles, ellipses, parabolas, or hyperbolas, or of any other curve

STYLES

DIFFERENT systems of construction have prevailed among different races, some employing only the Beam and Column, some also the Arch and Vault. In the choice of moldings, also, some have adopted one set of forms, some another. The forms employed by the Greeks and Romans constitute what are called the Classical Styles; those used in the Middle Ages, the Byzantine, Romanesque, and Gothic Styles. Some of the Gothic moldings have special names, such as Boltel, Scroll, etc.

At the close of the Middle Ages, about four hundred years ago, the Classical styles were revived, as the Medieval styles have been during the last hundred years. Both are now in use. The styles of Egypt, India, and China are employed only occasionally and as a matter of curiosity.

THE ORDERS

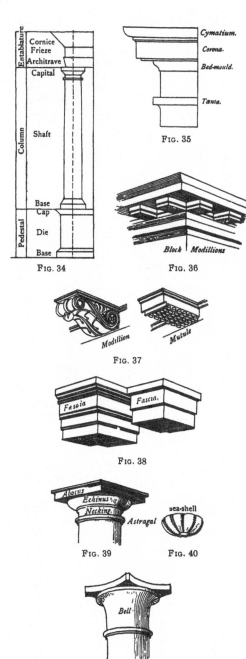

In the Classical styles, several varieties of Column and Entablature are in use. These are called the *Orders*. Each Order, Fig. 34, comprises a Column with Base, Shaft, and Capital, with or without a Pedestal, with its Base, Die, and Cap, and is crowned by an Entablature, consisting of Architrave, Frieze, and Cornice. The Entablature is generally about one-fourth as high as the Column, and the Pedestal one-third, more or less.

The principal member of the Cornice is the Corona, Fig. 35. Above the Corona, the Cornice is regularly terminated by a member originally designed to serve as a gutter to receive the water running down the roof. It generally consists of a large Cyma Recta, though the Ovolo and the Cavetto are often used. It is called the *Cymatium*, in spite of its large size, and whatever its shape.

NOTE.—The word *Cymatium* thus has three meanings: (1) A small Cyma. (2) A small crowning member, of whatever shape, though it is most frequently a Cyma Reversa. (3) The upper member of a Cornice, occupying the place of a gutter, whatever its shape, though it is generally a large Cyma Recta. In Classical Architecture, the Cyma Recta seldom occurs, except at the top of the Cornice and at the bottom of the Pedestal.

It would seem as if a cornice that occurs at the top of a wall and carries the edge of a roof would properly have a Cymatium, this being the place for a gutter, and that Cornices used as String Courses, half way up a wall, would naturally be without this member. But the significance of the Cymatium has frequently been overlooked, in ancient times and in modern. Many Greek temples have a Cymatium on the sloping lines of the gable, where a gutter would be useless, Fig. 120, and none along the Eaves, and in many modern buildings the cornices are crowned by large Cymatia in places where there are no roofs behind them.

The Corona is supported by a Molding or group of Moldings, called the *Bed Mold*. A row of brackets, termed *Blocks*, Fig. 36, *Modillions*, or *Mutules*, Fig. 37, according to their shape, resting on the Bed Mold and supporting the soffit of the Corona, is often added. At the top of the Architrave is a projecting molding that, when square, is called a *Tænia*, and the face of the Architrave is often broken up into two or three Bands or Fascias, Fig. 38, each of which often carries a small molding as a Cymatium or covering member.

The Abacus of the Capital also has a sort of bed mold beneath it, which, when convex, is called an *Echinus*, Fig. 39, from the sea shell, Fig. 40, which it resembles in shape. The little Frieze below it is called the *Necking*. But if the

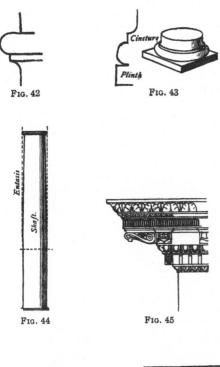

FIG. 42   FIG. 43

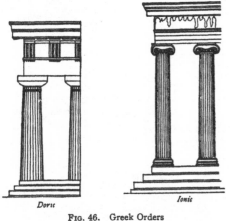

FIG. 44   FIG. 45

FIG. 46.   Greek Orders

FIG. 47.   Roman Orders

bed mold under the Abacus is concave, it dies into the necking like a large Congé, and the two together constitute the *Bell* of the Capital, Fig. 41. The Abacus is square in plan, but the Echinus, or the Bell below it, is round, like the column.

At the top of the shaft is a member called the *Astragal*, consisting of a Bead, Fillet, and Congé. It has a flat surface on top, as wide as the projection of the Congé, Fig. 42. At the bottom of the shaft is another Congé, called the *Apophyge*, below which is a broad fillet called the *Cincture*, Fig. 43. The Base generally has, below the base moldings, a plain member called the *Plinth*, which is square in plan like the Abacus.

The Shaft diminishes as it rises, Fig. 44, and the outline is not straight, but curved. This curve, which is called the *Entasis*, or bending, as of a bow, generally begins one-third of the way up, the lower third being cylindrical. The Entasis is not to be confounded with the *Diminution*, which is generally one-sixth, the upper Diameter being five-sixths of the lower.

The Pedestal also generally has a Corona and Bed Mold, but no gutter, and sometimes a Frieze, or Necking, above the Die, and a Base Molding and Plinth below it.

In the choice and use of moldings, the tastes and fashions of the Greeks and Romans were quite contrary to those of their successors in the Middle Ages. The Ancients preferred to use vertical and horizontal surfaces at right angles to each other, and seldom used an oblique line, or an acute or obtuse angle, as the Gothic architects did. They also preferred the Cyma Reversa, seldom employing the Cyma Recta, which in the Middle Ages was rather the favorite. Moreover, as has been said, the Gothic architects, in decorating a corner or edge, often cut it away to get a molding, but the Ancients raised the molding above the plane of the surface to which it was applied. In the composition and sequence of moldings also, the Classical architects generally avoid repetition, alternating large and small, plain and curved, convex and concave. The convex and concave profiles seldom describe an arc of more than 180 degrees, and except in the case of the Beak Molding and of the Bead, moldings are always separated by Fillets. When a molding is enriched, it is generally by carving ornamental forms, Fig. 45, upon it which resemble its own profile. The Greeks frequently employed elliptical and hyperbolic profiles, while the Romans generally used arcs of circles.

Among the Greeks, the forms, Fig. 46, used by the Doric race, which inhabited Greece itself and had colonies in Sicily and Italy, were much unlike those of the Ionic race, which inhabited the western coast of Asia Minor, and whose art was greatly influenced by that of Assyria and Persia. The Romans modified the *Ionic* and *Doric* styles, Fig. 47, and also devised a third, which was much more elaborate than either of them, and employed brackets, called *Modillions*, in the Cornice. This they called the *Corinthian*, Fig. 48. They used also a simpler Doric called the *Tuscan*, Fig. 49, and a cross between the Corinthian and Ionic called the *Composite*, Fig. 50. These are the *Five Orders*. The ancient examples vary much among themselves and differ in different places, and in modern times still further varieties are found in Italy, Spain, France, Germany, and England.

The best known and most admired forms for the Orders are those worked out by Giacomo Barozzi da Vignola, in the 16th century, from the study of ancient examples. The Orders that are shown in the large Plates almost exactly follow Vignola's rules.

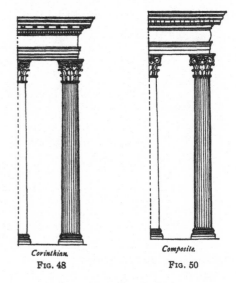

Corinthian.
FIG. 48

Composite.
FIG. 50

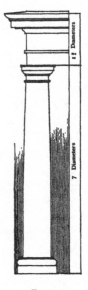

Tuscan
FIG. 49

VIGNOLA'S ORDERS—PLATE II

PLATE II shows the proportions of the Orders according to Vignola, in terms of the lower diameter of the columns. These vary in height from seven diameters to ten.

Note.—It is worth noting that, in ordinary handwriting, the T, for Tuscan, looks like a 7; D, for Doric, like an 8; I, for Ionic, like a 9; Co, for Corinthian and Composite reminds one of 10.

The Entablature is in all of them ordinarily one-fourth the height of the column, but it is sometimes made as small as one-fifth. The projection of the Cornice is the same as its height, except in the Doric Order, where it is greater. The lower band of the Architrave is made to come in line with the upper face of the shaft.

But it is only when seen in elevation that these relations obtain. When seen in perspective, as is generally the case, the cornice appears much larger, in proportion, and the frieze and architrave, being foreshortened, much smaller, and the architrave overhangs the shaft, Figs. 53 and 57.

In the Greek Orders, the Column is from five to ten diameters in height and the Entablature always about two diameters. In the Greek Orders, accordingly, the taller the Column, the lighter the Entablature, relatively; but in the Roman Orders, the taller the Column, the heavier the Entablature, actually. It follows that the weight of the Greek Entablature is proportioned to the diameter of the Column, irrespective of its height; of the Roman to the height of the Column, regardless of its diameter. The Romans put the least weight on the shortest and strongest supports. The Greek plan shows more regard to principles of construction, the Roman to principles of decorative composition.

Vignola used half of the lower diameter of the Column as his unit of measure, or *Module*. This he divided into twelve Parts for the Tuscan and Doric Orders, and into eighteen Minutes for the others, and he gives all the dimensions both of the larger members and of the moldings in terms of Modules and Parts, or Minutes, sometimes using even the quarter Minute, or one one-hundred-and-forty-fourth of a Diameter. But it is equally practicable and more convenient to use the whole *Diameter* as a unit of measure, dividing it only into Fourths and Sixths, and occasionally using an Eighth or a Twelfth.

In Plates IV, VI, VII, IX, XI, and XIII, the first column on the left shows the vertical dimensions as given in Plate II. In the second column, these divisions are subdivided into equal parts, the third column giving a further division of the dimensions thus obtained. Most of these dimensions can be stated in terms of sixths or fourths of the Diameter, as appears in the Tables. This analysis does not reach the smaller details, the shape and size of which must be learned by observation. Indeed, all these forms should be made so familiar that they can be drawn accurately from memory, these arithmetical relations being used only to test the accuracy of the result, or to discover how much the proportions adopted in any given case differ from the regular type. For Vignola's Orders are to be regarded only as an admirable standard that may be safely adopted when there is no occasion to do anything else, but which is to be departed from and varied whenever there is any reason for doing so. Vignola obviously so regarded them. He did not himself adhere closely to his own rules, or generally adopt his Orders in his own work. His Doric and Ionic are to be found, however, in the Villa Caprarola.

THE TUSCAN ORDER—PLATES III AND IV

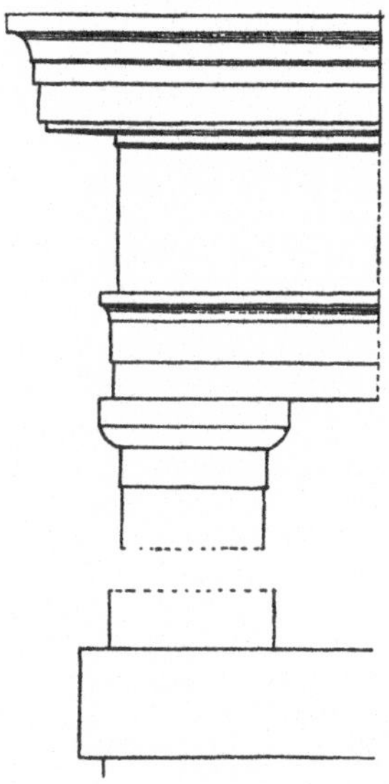

Temple of Piety

FIG. 51

THE distinguishing characteristics of the Tuscan Order is simplicity. Any forms of Pedestal, Column, and Entablature that show but few moldings, and those plain, are considered to be Tuscan. Such are, in antiquity, those of the Temple of Piety in Rome, Fig. 51, and the lower order of the Amphitheater at Arles. Vignola's Tuscan Order, Fig. 52, is marked by the use of the Ovolo in the Cymatium, and by the frequent employment of the Congé. The height of the Column is seven Diameters and that of the Entablature accordingly seven-quarters, or a Diameter and three-quarters. The Base, Capital, Architrave, and Frieze are each half a Diameter high, and the Cornice three-quarters. But this measurement includes not only the Base itself, but the Cincture at the foot of the Shaft. Dividing the Cornice into four parts, the Capitals into three, and the Base into two, gives the principal horizontal divisions. The Bed Mold is a large Cyma Reversa. The Abacus is seven-sixths of a Diameter across, not including the Fillet at the top, and it projects its own height from the face of the Architrave above, which is in line with the Necking below.

All the principal dimensions can be expressed in terms of fourths and sixths of the lower Diameter of the Shaft.

Vignola makes the width of the Plinth a little greater than this, and sets the Bed Mold up one-twelfth, making the Frieze wider and the Corona narrower.

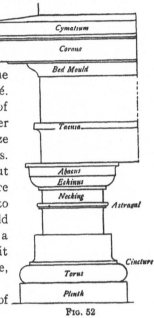

FIG. 52

TABLE OF THE TUSCAN ORDER—PLATES III AND IV

$\frac{1}{4} D$ equals height of Plinth.

$\frac{3}{4} D$ "   height of Cornice.

      "   projection of Cornice.

$\frac{1}{6} D$ "   height of Necking.

      "   height of Echinus.

      "   height of Abacus.

$\frac{1}{2} D = \frac{3}{6} D$ "   height of Base, including Cincture.

      "   height of Capital.

      "   height of Architrave.

      "   height of Frieze.

$\frac{5}{6} D$ "   upper Diameter of Shaft.

$\frac{6}{6} D$ "   lower Diameter of Shaft.

$\frac{7}{6} D$ "   width of Abacus.

$\frac{8}{6} D$ "   width of Plinth.

$\frac{1}{12} D$ "   width and projection of Tænia.

$\frac{1}{16} D$ "   height of Astragal and projection of Astragal.

THE DORIC ORDER—PLATES V, VI, AND VII

THE distinguishing characteristics of the Doric Order, Figs. 53 and 54, are features in the Frieze and in the Bed Mold above it, called *Triglyphs* and *Mutules*, which are supposed to be derived from the ends of beams and rafters in a primitive wooden construction with large beams. Under each Triglyph, and beneath the Tænia that crowns the Architrave, is a little Fillet called the *Regula*. Under the Regula are six long drops, called *Guttæ*, which are sometimes conical, sometimes pyramidal. There are also either eighteen or thirty-six short cylindrical Guttæ under the soffit of each Mutule. The Guttæ are supposed to represent the heads of wooden pins, or treenails.

Two different Doric Orders are in use, the *Mutulary*, Figs. 53, 54, and 55, and the *Denticulated*, Figs. 56, 57, and 58. They differ chiefly in the cornices. In both of them the height, of three-quarters of a Diameter, is divided into four equal parts, the upper one embracing the gutter, or Cymatium, and the Fillet below, the next the Corona and the small Cyma Reversa, or Cymatium, above it. But the Bed Molds are unlike. In both of them, the lower member of the Bed Mold is a broad fillet, a sort of Upper Tænia, called the *Cap of the Triglyph*. This, unlike the Tænia below, breaks around the angles of the Triglyph, serving as a sort of crowning member, or cymatium, to both the Triglyph and the Metope.

In the Mutulary Doric, above the Cap of the Triglyph, is a narrow fillet that does not break around the angles and accordingly shows a broad soffit over the Metopes and at the corner of the building. These two fillets occupy the lower half of the lower quarter of the cornice. The upper half of the lower quarter, above this little fillet, is an Ovolo, and above this, the second quarter of the Cornice is occupied by a broad Fascia, called the *Mutule Band*, upon which are planted the *Mutules*, one over each Triglyph, which are half a Diameter wide, like the Triglyphs below them. They are broad, low, oblong brackets crowned with a Fillet and Cyma Reversa, which also crown the Mutule Band between the brackets. On the soffit of each Mutule are thirty-six Guttæ and a drip molding.

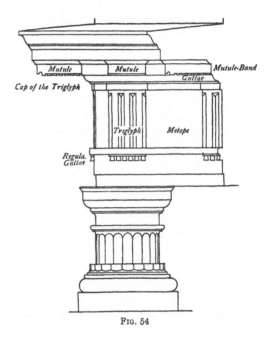

FIG. 54

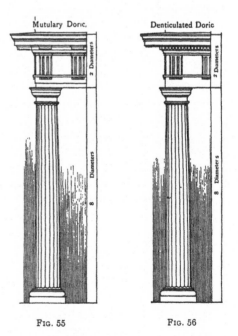

FIG. 55　　　FIG. 56

FIG. 57

FIG. 53

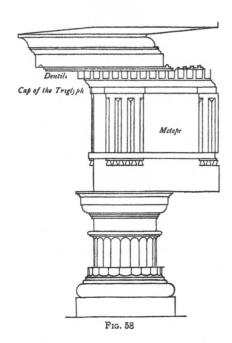

FIG. 58

In the Denticulated Doric, Figs. 56, 57, and 58, the place of the Fillet and Ovolo above the Cap of the Triglyph is taken by a large Cyma Reversa, the soffit of which is wider over the Metopes than over the Triglyphs, as is that of the small Fillet in the Mutulary. Above this molding is a band like the Mutule Band, but instead of brackets, extending out under the Corona, it bears a row of small blocks, like teeth called *Dentils*. These are one-eighth of a Diameter high, and are set one-eighth of a Diameter from center to center, or edge to edge. If this last dimension is divided into thirds, two of these go to the Dentil, and one to the space between it and the next one. This space is called an *Interdentil*, which is accordingly one twenty-fourth of a Diameter wide. The Dentil is thus one-eighth of a Diameter long and one-twelfth wide, or half a sixth, or of the proportions of two to three, like the Triglyph. The face of the last Dentil on the corner and the side of the first one around the corner come together in elevation without any Interdentil, giving the appearance of a *Double Dentil*, for the Dentils are square in plan and the side is just as wide as the face.

As the Triglyphs are a Diameter and a quarter on centers, or ten-eighths, there are ten Dentils to each Triglyph and Metope.

A Dentil comes just over the axis of each Column and there are three Dentils between the one over the corner Column and the Double Dentil on the corner, the farther edge of the third one being just over the face of the Frieze, or five-twelfths of a Diameter from the axis of the Column.

The last Dentil, or first half of the Double Dentil, is centered over the outer face of the bottom of the shaft, Fig. 92.

The Dentils constitute the upper member of the Bed Mold. They leave the chief part of the Corona unsupported, but the soffit of the Corona, which is slightly inclined, recalling the slope of the rafters, is not so wide as the soffit of the Mutulary Doric, owing to this encroachment of the Dentils. The Mutules, which are very shallow, have, accordingly, only eighteen Guttæ in place of thirty-six; that is, three rows instead of six. There is also a Mutule over each Metope, as well as one over each Triglyph.

Vignola gives his Denticulated Doric a large Cavetto for a Cymatium, or gutter, instead of a Cyma Recta, and supports the Echinus of the Capital by three fillets, instead of by a Fillet and Bead, Fig. 58.

The Triglyphs are three-quarters of a Diameter high and half a Diameter wide, Fig. 59. This width is divided into three parts, called *Shanks*. Each Shank, or *Femur*, is beveled on the edge nearly up to the top of the Triglyph, making in all two channels and two half channels. Each Shank is one-sixth of a Diameter wide and each beveled face a quarter of a sixth. The plain face of the Shank is, accordingly, one-twelfth, and just as wide as the channel. These are almost the only beveled faces to be found in the whole range of Classical Architecture, though beveled fillets are not uncommon. The two full channels are generally cut in at an angle of 45 degrees, but the two half channels on either side are shallower, and do not reach the face of the Frieze.

The Triglyphs come just over the Columns. The portion of the Frieze between the Triglyphs is called a *Metope*. It is exactly square, being three-quarters of a Diameter wide. The fragment of a Metope between the last Triglyph and the corner of the Frieze is one-sixth of a Diameter wide. The face of the Metopes comes over the lower band of the Architrave, and that of the Triglyph projects slightly beyond the face of the upper Band.

The Column is eight Diameters in height, the Base, Capital, and Architrave each half a Diameter, the Frieze and Cornice each three-quarters. The total projection of the Cornice, including the Cymatium, is one Diameter. The Architrave is divided into two Bands, or Fascias. The lower one occupies the lower third of the Architrave, and the Tænia, Regula, and Guttæ the upper third. Half of this third goes to the Tænia, the projection of which equals its height.

The Doric Column has twenty *Channels*, each about one-sixth of a Diameter wide, which show in section, Fig. 60, an arc of 60 degrees. The solid edge that separates them, called the *Arris*, makes an angle of something over 90 degrees (102 degrees). The ten Arrises shown in elevation are easy to draw, as two come on the outline of the Shaft, two come on its "corners," and the two middle ones are almost exactly one-sixth of a Diameter apart. The channels are .157 of a Diameter wide, so that making the middle one-sixth, or .166 of a Diameter, involves an error of only .009 of a Diameter, or about one-eighteenth of its width. The four other Arrises can then be put in without much difficulty.

The Doric Base and Capital, Figs. 54 and 58, are divided, like the Tuscan, into halves and thirds, but with additional moldings, a bead being added above the Torus of the Base, and another below the Echinus of the Capital. The Abacus is crowned by a cymatium consisting of a Fillet and Cyma Reversa. If the height of the Capital is divided into thirds, each of the two upper thirds again into thirds, and the upper and lower of these still again into three equal parts, all the horizontal lines of the Capital will be determined, as shown in Plate V. The base, including the Cincture, as in the Tuscan Order, is half a Diameter high.

Vignola's Denticulated Doric is imitated closely from the Doric Order of the Theater of Marcellus, and the Mutulary, which he has been thought to have invented, seems to have been derived from the Doric Order of the Basilica Julia, Fig. 61. There are no Roman Doric temples.

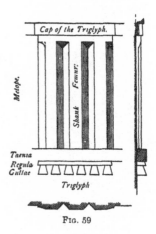

Fig. 59

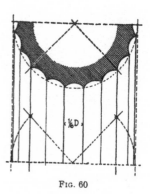

Fig. 60

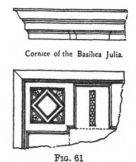

Cornice of the Basilica Julia.

Fig. 61

TABLE OF THE DORIC ORDER—PLATES V, VI, AND VII

$\frac{3}{4}D$ equals height of Frieze.
      "   height of Cornice.
      "   projection of Corona (Denticulated).
      "   projection of Mutule (Mutulary).
      "   width of Metope.

$\frac{1}{4}D$ "   height of Plinth.
$\frac{1}{6}D$ "   projection of Plinth.
      "   projection of Abacus.
      "   height of Abacus.
      "   height of Necking.
      "   height of Echinus and Bead.
      "   height of Lower Band.
      "   height of Guttæ, Regula, and Tænia.
      "   width of Shank.
      "   width of Corner Metope.

$\frac{1}{2}D = \frac{3}{6}D$ "   height of Base, including the Cincture.
      "   height of Capital.
      "   height of Architrave.
      "   width of Triglyph.

$\frac{1}{8}D$ "   height of Dentils.
      "   distance of Dentils o. c.
$\frac{1}{12}D$ "   width of Dentils.
      "   height of Tænia.
      "   projection of Tænia.

$\frac{1}{16}D$ "   height of Astragal.
      "   projection of Astragal.

$\frac{1}{24}D$ "   width of Interdentils.

THE IONIC ORDER—PLATES VIII AND IX

THE prototypes of the Ionic Order are to be found in
Persia, Assyria, Fig. 62, and Asia Minor. Like the Doric
Order, it seems to have originated in a wooden construction.
It is characterized by Bands in the Architrave and Dentils
in the Bed Mold, both of which are held to represent sticks
laid together to form a beam or a roof. But the most conspicuous and distinctive feature is the *Scrolls* that decorate
the Capital of the Column. These have no structural sig-
nificance, and are purely decorative forms derived from
Assyria and Egypt. Originally the Ionic Order had no
Frieze and no Echinus in the Capital. These were borrowed
from the Doric Order, and, in like manner, the Dentils and
Bands in the Doric were imitated from the Ionic. The Ionic
Frieze was introduced in order to afford a place for sculpture, and was called by the Greeks the *Zoöphorus*, or Figure
Bearer, Fig. 64.

In the Ionic Entablature, the Architrave, Frieze, and
Cornice are about the same height, each measuring about
three-quarters of a Diameter. But Vignola makes the Architrave a little smaller and the Cornice a little larger, so that
they measure, respectively, five-eighths, six-eighths, and seven-
eighths of a Diameter. The Architrave is divided into five
parts, each an eighth of a Diameter in height. The upper one
is occupied by a large Cyma Reversa and Fillet, which take
the place of the Doric Tænia. Below are two facias, or
bands, of equal height, each measuring a quarter of a Diameter. The lower one is crowned by an Ovolo and Fillet.
The French often use three bands, as in the Corinthian
Architrave.

The Ionic Frieze is plain, except for the sculpture upon it.
It sometimes has a curved outline, as if ready to be carved,
and is then said to be *Pulvinated*, from *Pulvinar*, a bolster,
which it much resembles.

The Cornice is much like that of the Denticulated Doric,
which was derived from it, but has no Mutules. The upper
half, as in the Doric, is taken up by the Cymatium and
Corona, and the lower half by the Bed Mold.

This is divided into four equal parts, of which the upper
one is given to an Ovolo, the lower to a Cyma Reversa and
Fillet, and the two middle ones to a Dentil Band and Fillet.
Upon this band are planted the Dentils, which are one-sixth

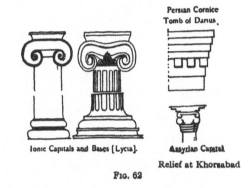

Ionic Capitals and Bases [Lycia].

Persian Cornice
Tomb of Darius.

Assyrian Capital
Relief at Khorsabad

FIG. 62

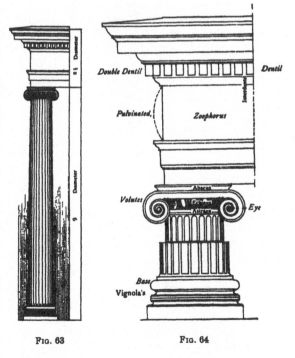

FIG. 63

FIG. 64

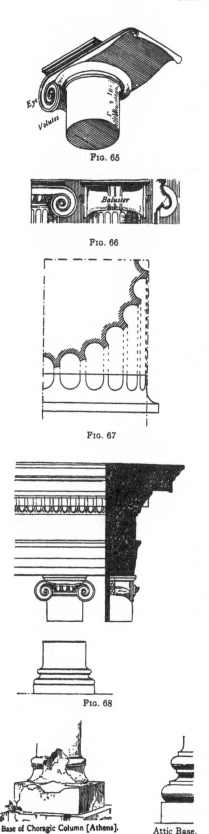

FIG. 65

FIG. 66

FIG. 67

FIG. 68

Base of Choragic Column [Athens].

FIG. 69

Attic Base.

FIG. 70

of a Diameter high, and are set one-sixth on centers, or on edges, instead of one-eighth, as in the Denticulated Doric. Two-thirds of this sixth go to the width of the Dentil and one to the space between, or Interdentil. The Dentil is, accordingly, one-ninth of a Diameter wide, and the Interdentil one-eighteenth, instead of a twelfth and a twenty-fourth. A Dentil is put on the axis of a column, and an Interdentil comes just over the outer line of the Frieze. There is, apparently, a Double Dentil on the corner, the outer face of which is two-thirds of a Diameter, or four-sixths, from the axis of the column. The first half of it, as in the Denticulated Doric, comes over the outer face of the lower end of the shaft, Fig. 93. There are two Dentils between the one over the column and the Double Dentil, in place of three, as in the Doric.

The Ionic Capital, like the Doric, has an Echinus and an Abacus crowned by a Cyma Reversa and Fillet. But generally it has no Necking, and it is, accordingly, only two-sixths of a Diameter in height, or one-third instead of one-half. Both the Echinus and the Cymatium that crowns the Abacus are larger than in the Doric, and the face of the Abacus smaller, and the Echinus projects in front of the Abacus, instead of being covered by it. The Abacus and its Fillet extend beyond the Echinus on either side, and are curled up into the Scrolls, or *Volutes*, Fig. 65, the whole height of which is a half Diameter, measuring down from the Architrave. The *Eyes* of the Scrolls are one-third of a Diameter from the top, on the line separating the bottom of the Capital from the top of the Astragal that crowns the Shaft. They are just one Diameter apart on centers, coming over the outer lines of the lower end of the Shaft, and the inner edges of the Scrolls are two-thirds apart. The Echinus is generally carved with Eggs and Darts, three of which show between the Scrolls, the next one on either side being hidden by sprigs of Honeysuckle Ornament. These Scrolls, Fig. 66, show on the sides a series of moldings called the *Baluster*, or *Bolster*. The term Abacus is generally held to apply only to the Cyma Reversa and Fillet, above the Scrolls.

The Shaft of the column is ornamented with twenty-four *Flutings*, Fig. 67, semicircular in section, which are separated not by an Arris, but by a Fillet of about one-fourth their width. This makes the Flutings only about two-thirds as wide as the Doric Channels, or about one-ninth of a Diameter, instead of one-sixth. Four-fifths of one twenty-fourth of the circumference is .106 of a Diameter, while one-ninth of the Diameter is .111, a difference of less than a twentieth.

The typical Ionic base is considered to consist mainly of a Scotia, as in some Greek examples, Fig. 69. It is common, however, to use instead what is called the *Attic Base*, Fig. 70, consisting of a Scotia and two Fillets between two large Toruses, mounted on a Plinth, the whole half a Diameter high. The Plinth occupies the lower third, or one-sixth of

a Diameter. Vignola adopted for his Ionic Order a modifi-
cation of the Attic Base, substituting for the single large
Scotia two small ones, separated by one or two Beads and
Fillets and omitting the lower Torus, Fig. 64.

The principal ancient examples of the Ionic Order in Rome
are those of the Theater of Marcellus, Fig. 71, and of the
Temple of Fortuna Virilis, Fig. 72.

The Ionic Capital sometimes has a necking like the Doric,
which is then generally decorated, Fig. 73. Sometimes, also,
the four faces of the Capital are made alike, double scrolls
occurring at the corners, where they project at an angle of
45 degrees. In this case there is no Baluster, and the Capital resembles the upper portion of a Composite Capital. It
is then sometimes called the Roman Ionic Capital, or the
Scamozzi Capital, Fig. 74, from the name of the architect,
Scamozzi, who frequently employed it.

Almost all the dimensions of the Ionic Order can be
expressed in terms of sixths of a Diameter, as appears in
the following Table:

Theatre of Marcellus

FIG. 71

Temple of Fortuna Virilis

FIG. 72

Scamozzi Capital

FIG. 74

Roman Capital [in the Lateran Museum].

FIG. 73

TABLE OF THE IONIC ORDER—PLATES VIII AND IX

$\frac{5}{8} D$ equals height of Architrave.

$\frac{3}{4} D = \frac{6}{8} D$ "   height of Frieze.

$\frac{7}{8} D$ "   height of Cornice.

  "   projection of Cornice.

$\frac{1}{4} D = \frac{2}{8} D$ "   height of each Band.

$\frac{1}{6} D$ "   projection of Plinth.

  "   height of Plinth.

  "   height of Dentils.

  "   distance of Dentils, o. c.

  "   projection of Abacus.

$\frac{1}{3} D = \frac{2}{6} D$ "   height of Capital.

$\frac{1}{2} D = \frac{3}{6} D$ "   height of Base.

  "   height of Scrolls.

$\frac{2}{3} D = \frac{4}{6} D$ "   distance between Scrolls.

  "   distance from Axis to outer face of Double Dentil.

$\frac{5}{6} D$ "   upper Diameter.

$1 D = \frac{6}{6} D$ "   lower Diameter.

  "   distance of Eyes of Scrolls, o. c.

  "   length of Baluster.

$\frac{7}{6} D$ "   width of Abacus.

$1\frac{1}{3} D = \frac{8}{6} D$ "   width of Plinth.

  "   width of Echinus (minus).

$1\frac{1}{2} D = \frac{9}{6} D$ "   width of Scrolls (minus).

$\frac{1}{6} D$ "   width of Dentil.

  "   width of Flúting.

$\frac{1}{12} D$ "   height of Astragal.

  "   projection of Astragal.

$\frac{1}{18} D$ "   width of Interdentil.

THE CORINTHIAN ORDER—PLATES X AND XI

THE three distinguishing characteristics of the Corinthian
Order, Fig. 75, are a tall bell-shaped Capital, a series of small
brackets, called *Modillions*, that support the Cornice instead
of Mutules, in addition to the Dentils, and a general richness
of detail, which is enhanced by the use of the *Acanthus leaf*,
Fig. 76, in both Capitals and Modillions.

The height of the Cornice, Fig. 77, is divided into five
parts. The two lower and the two upper parts resemble the
lower and upper halves of the Ionic Cornice. The middle
fifth is occupied by a *Modillion Band*, which carries the
Modillions, or brackets. These, as well as the Modillion band,
are crowned by a small Cyma Reversa. They consist of a
double scroll, beneath which is an Acanthus leaf. Each
Modillion is five-twelfths of a Diameter long; i. e., half the
upper Diameter of the Shaft, one-fifth high, and as wide as
a Dentil and two Interdentils; that is to say, two-ninths of
a Diameter. They are set two-thirds of a Diameter on centers,
one being over the axis of the corner Column, and one over
the outer face of the Double Dentil. The soffit of the Corona
between the Modillions is occupied by a sinkage with moldings,
called a *Caisson*, in the middle of which there is a large
Rosette. The Caisson is twice as wide as the Modillion; i. e.,
four-ninths of a Diameter.

As the Modillions are two-thirds of a Diameter on centers,
or four-sixths, and the Dentils are one-sixth, on centers, it
follows that there are four Dentils to each Modillion; i. e., a
Dentil under every Modillion, and three between. As in
the Ionic Order and in the Denticulated Doric, the last
Dentil, which is the first half of the Double Dentil, is centered over the face of the lower Diameter of the column,
Fig. 94.

The Architrave, which is three-quarters of a Diameter high,
has three Bands and a large cymatium, which is as wide as
the first Band. The two lower Bands occupy the lower half
of the Architrave, and the third Band and the cymatium
the upper. A small Bead, or a small Cyma Reversa, generally crowns each Band. The Frieze, which is also three-
quarters of a Diameter high, may be plain, pulvinated, or
sculptured.

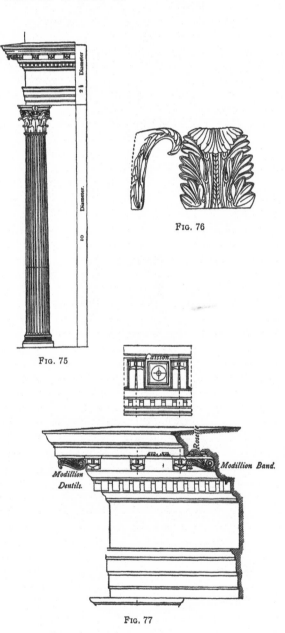

FIG. 75

FIG. 76

FIG. 77

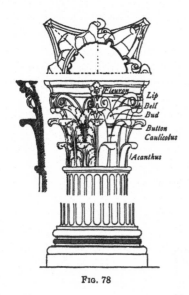

FIG. 78

FIG. 79

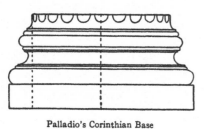

Palladio's Corinthian Base

FIG. 80

The Capital, Fig. 78, is seven-sixths of a Diameter high, the upper sixth being taken up by the Abacus, which is nine-sixths, or a Diameter and a half, in width, though it does not look so. It is molded on the edge with an Ovolo and Fillet above a large Congé and small Fascia. The corners are cut off at an angle of 45 degrees, and the sides hollowed out in a curve of 60 degrees. The width across from curve to curve is seven-sixths of a Diameter. Each face of the Abacus bears a flower, called the *Fleuron*, that springs from a small bud above the middle leaf.

The *Bell* of the capital, Fig. 79, is one Diameter high, or six-sixths; it terminates under the Abacus in a Beak Molding called the *Lip of the Bell*, which measures seven-sixths of a Diameter across, its greatest projection coming just under the least projection of the upper line of the Abacus. The lower two-sixths are covered by a row of eight Acanthus leaves, which bend down at the top to the extent of half a sixth, or a quarter of their own height. The next two-sixths show a similar row of eight leaves, set alternately with those below, four facing the sides of the Capital, and four the corners. Like those of the first row, they spring from the Astragal at the top of the Shaft, and the mid-rib of each leaf shows between two lower leaves, it being really four-sixths high. These also bend down half a sixth. Between the eight leaves of the second row are eight *Caulicoli*, or cabbage stalks, which terminate in a *Button*, upon which rests a sort of *Bud*, which divides into two leaves. These turn right and left, the larger one toward the corner of the Capital, the smaller toward the side or front under the Fleuron. From each Bud rise also two scrolls, or Volutes, one of which runs out to support the projecting corner of the Abacus. The other, which is smaller, and does not rise higher than the Lip of the Bell, supports the Fleuron. Sixteen leaves of a third row curl over under these sixteen volutes, making with them eight masses of ornament, one on each corner of the column, and one in the middle of each side. These give in plan an eight-pointed star, each point consisting of a large leaf, two small leaves, two Volutes, and above them, either the Fleuron or the horn of the Abacus. Between them is seen the Bell of the Cap, with its Lip.

Here, again, the Attic Base is commonly used, but sometimes, especially in large columns, a base is used that resembles Vignola's Ionic Base, with two Beads between the Scotias, except that it has a lower Torus, Fig. 78. Palladio uses a very elegant variety of Attic Base, enriched by the addition of Beads and Fillets, Fig. 80. The Shaft is fluted like the Ionic shaft, with twenty-four semicircular flutings, but these are sometimes filled with a convex molding, or *Cable*, to a third of their height, Fig. 75.

Almost all the buildings erected by the Romans employ the Corinthian Order.

TABLE OF THE CORINTHIAN ORDER—PLATES X AND XI

$\frac{3}{4} D$ equals height of Architrave.

     "   height of Frieze.

$1 D = \frac{4}{4} D$ "   height of Cornice.

     "   projection of Cornice.

$\frac{1}{8} D$ "   projection of Plinth.

     "   height of Plinth.

     "   height of Lower Band.

     "   height of Dentils.

     "   distance of Dentils, o. c.

$\frac{1}{3} D = \frac{3}{8} D$ "   height of Leaves.

     "   projection of Abacus.

$\frac{2}{3} D = \frac{4}{8} D$ "   distance of Modillions, o. c.

     "   distance from Axis to face of Double Dentil.

$\frac{5}{6} D$ "   upper Diameter.

$1 D = \frac{6}{8} D$ "   lower Diameter.

     "   height of Bell.

     "   height of Cornice.

     "   projection of Cornice.

$\frac{7}{6} D$ "   height of Capital.

     "   width of Abacus (least).

     "   width of Lip of the Bell.

$1\frac{1}{3} D = \frac{8}{6} D$ "   width of Plinth.

$1\frac{1}{2} D = \frac{9}{6} D$ "   width of Abacus (greatest).

$2 D = \frac{12}{6} D$ "   width of Abacus (diagonal).

$\frac{4}{3} D$ "   width of Caisson.

$\frac{1}{6} D$ "   width of Dentil.

$\frac{2}{6} D$ "   width of Modillion.

$\frac{1}{18} D$ "   width of Interdentil.

$\frac{1}{12} D$ "   height of Astragal.

     "   projection of Astragal.

$\frac{5}{12} D$ "   length of Modillion.

$\frac{1}{6} D$ "   height of Modillion.

THE COMPOSITE ORDER—PLATES XII AND XIII

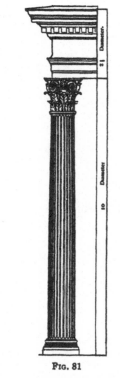

FIG. 81

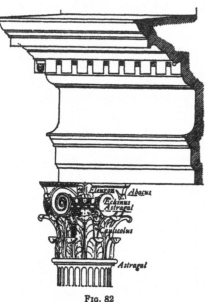

FIG. 82

THE Composite Order, Fig. 81, is a heavier Corinthian, just as the Tuscan is a simplified Doric. The chief proportions are the same as in the Corinthian Order, but the details are fewer and larger. It owes its name to the Capital, Fig. 82, in which the two lower rows of leaves and the Caulicoli are the same as in the Corinthian. But the Caulicoli carry only a stunted leaf-bud, and the upper row of leaves and the sixteen Volutes are replaced by the large Scrolls, Echinus, and Astragal of a complete Ionic Capital, with four faces like Scamozzi's. A Composite Capital thus has two Astragals, if the lower be included, but this properly belongs to the shaft. The Scrolls are nearly half a Diameter high, covering up half the Abacus and coming down so as to touch the second row of Acanthus leaves. They measure fully nine-sixths across, and are only three-sixths apart, or half a Diameter, instead of four-sixths, as in the Ionic.

Vignola's Composite Entablature, Fig. 82, differs from his Ionic chiefly in the shape and size of the Dentils. They are larger, and are more nearly square in elevation, being a fifth of a Diameter high, and one-sixth wide, the Interdentil being one-twelfth, and they are set one-fourth of a Diameter apart, on centers. The last Dentil, or first half of the Double Dentil, is centered over the outer face of the Column, at the bottom, as in the Corinthian, Ionic, and Denticulated Doric, Fig. 95. The outer face of the Double Dentil is three-quarters of a Diameter from the axis of the Column, and there is only one Dentil between the Double Dentil and the one over the axis, against two in the Corinthian and Ionic, and three in the Denticulated Doric. The Frieze terminates in a large Congé over the Architrave, and the Corona is undercut with a large quirked Cyma Recta, making a drip.

Palladio's Composite Entablature, Fig. 83, is more characteristic than Vignola's, the parts being fewer and larger. The Architrave has two Bands, the Frieze terminates in two large Congés, and the Cornice is divided into two equal parts, each half a Diameter high. The upper half is shared about equally by the Cymatium and the Corona, and the lower half is almost entirely taken up by a series of large brackets, or *Blocks*, a third of a Diameter high, and one-fourth wide, divided into two Bands. The inner face of the *Double Block* comes just in line with the Frieze below, Fig. 102. The bands and moldings that decorate the Blocks are continued between them.

These dimensions apply to Palladio's entablature where it is made of the same size as Vignola's, that is to say, a quarter of the height of the column, or two Diameters and a half. But Palladio himself made his Composite entablature only two Diameters high, or one-fifth of the length of the column, cutting down the Frieze to half a Diameter, the Architrave to two-thirds, and the Cornice to five-sixths. If the dimensions of Palladio's Cornice given in the table are, accordingly, taken from the upper diameter of the shaft instead of from the lower, they will exactly conform to Palladio's own usage.

The Block entablature used by Scamozzi for his Composite Order is even less than two Diameters in height, and this seems to have been the case also with the entablature of the Olympiæum at Athens, which Palladio is thought to have imitated.

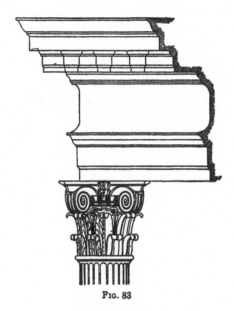

FIG. 83

The moldings below the Blocks are often made to project more than in Palladio's example. This increases their distance apart, on centers, since one must still come over the axis of the column and the one on the corner must be as far out as the end of these moldings. The Blocks also vary considerably in length in different examples.

The upper part of the Composite Capital, as has been said, is often used alone as a variety of the Ionic Capital.

The Composite Capital is employed in the Arch of Titus in Rome, and elsewhere, with a Corinthian entablature, and the Block Cornice occurs in the so-called frontispiece of Nero, as well as in the temple at Athens, in connection with a Corinthian Capital.

TABLE OF THE COMPOSITE ORDER—PLATES XII AND XIII

$\frac{1}{3} D = \frac{4}{8} D$ equals height of Scrolls.
          "   space between Scrolls.

$\frac{3}{4} D$ "   distance of Eyes, o. c.
$1\frac{1}{2} D = \frac{9}{8} D$ "   width of Scrolls.
          "   width of Plinth.
          "   width of Abacus.

VIGNOLA'S CORNICE

$\frac{1}{4} D$ "   height of Dentil Band.
     "   distance of Dentils, o. c.

$\frac{3}{4} D$ "   distance from Axis to face of Double Dentil.
$\frac{1}{6} D$ "   height of Dentils.
$\frac{1}{8} D$ "   width of Dentils.
$\frac{1}{16} D$ "   width of Interdentil.

PALLADIO'S CORNICE

$\frac{1}{8} D$ "   height of Block.
     "   length of Block.

$\frac{1}{5} D$ "   width of Block.
     "   height of Lower Band.
     "   height of Corona.
     "   height of Cymatium.
     "   distance between Blocks (*plus*).

GEOMETRICAL RELATIONS

THE dimensions and proportions set forth in the previous paragraphs, and recapitulated in the Tables, enable one to draw the Five Orders, according to Vignola, with great accuracy and sufficiently in detail for all the ordinary purposes of the draftsman and designer. The figures for the larger features are easily remembered, and the smaller divisions and subdivisions can for the most part be obtained by dividing the larger into two, three, four, or five equal parts.

But besides these arithmetical proportions some geometrical relations may be pointed out, which are calculated greatly to facilitate the work of draftsmanship, drawing being naturally more closely related to Geometry than to Arithmetic.

LINES AT 45 DEGREES

The proportions of any figure that is as wide as it is high, and which can accordingly be included within a square, are most easily determined by drawing the diagonal of the square, that is to say, by drawing a line with a 45-degree triangle. Such figures are, as is shown in the Illustrations, the projections of:

1. The Echinus, in the Tuscan, Doric, and Ionic Capitals, Figs. 84 and 85.
2. The Abacus, in the Tuscan and Doric Capitals, Figs. 84 and 85.
3. The Astragal, in all the Orders, Fig. 86.
4. The Architrave, including the Tænia, in the Tuscan and Doric Orders, counting from the axis of the Column, Figs. 84 and 85.
5. The Tænia itself, and the Cymatium that takes its place, Figs. 84 and 85.
6. All the Cornices, except the Doric, Fig. 84.

A line drawn at 45 degrees through the Doric Cornice from the top of the Frieze gives, where it cuts the upper line of the Cornice:

7. The face of the Corona, in the Denticulated Doric, Fig. 85.
8. The face of the Mutule, in the Mutulary Doric, Fig. 85.

A line drawn at 45 degrees through the Doric Architrave and Frieze, from a point on the axis of the Column and of the Triglyph, taken either at the bottom of the Architrave or at the top of the Frieze, gives:

9. The Axis of the next Triglyph, and so on, Fig. 85

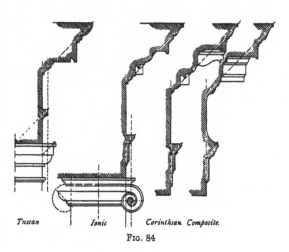

Tuscan   Ionic   Corinthian. Composite.

FIG. 84

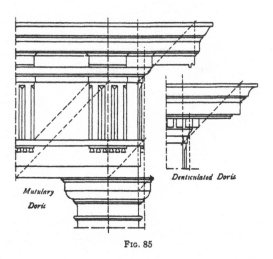

Mutulary Doric

Denticulated Doric

FIG. 85

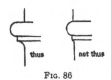

thus   not thus

FIG. 86

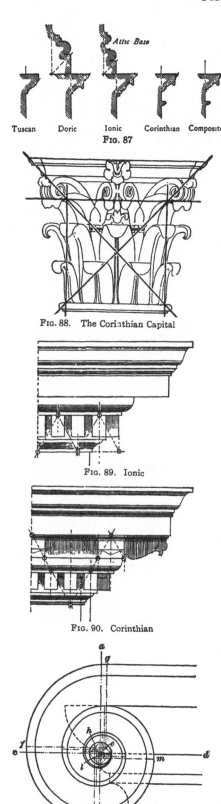

Tuscan   Doric   Ionic   Corinthian   Composite
FIG. 87

FIG. 88.   The Corinthian Capital

FIG. 89.   Ionic

FIG. 90.   Corinthian

FIG. 91.   The Ionic Capital

A 45-degree line also gives:

10.   The Shape of the Metope, Fig. 85.
11.   The Caps of the Pedestals, except the Tuscan, Fig. 87.
12.   The Plinths of the Doric and Attic Bases, Fig. 87.

Lines drawn at an angle of 45 degrees across the Corinthian Capital from the extremities of its lower diameter give:

13.   The width of the Abacus, Fig. 88.

Where they cut the line of the upper diameter of the shaft, extended, they give:

14.   The depth of the Scroll, Fig. 88.

LINES AT 60 DEGREES

In like manner, lines drawn at an angle of 60 degrees through the Bed Mold of the Ionic Cornice from a point on the axis of the Column, taken either on the upper line of the Frieze or on the upper edge of the Dentil Band, give, where they touch the upper line of the Frieze and the upper line of the Dentil Band:

15.   The Axes of the Dentils, and the outer face of the Double Dentil, Fig. 89.

Similar lines drawn at 60 degrees in the Corinthian Cornice, taken from a point where the axis of the Column cuts the lower edge of the Corona, give:

(*a*)   Where they cut the lower edge of the Corona, the upper line of the Frieze, and the lower line of the Ovolo:

16.   The Axes of the Modillions and of the Dentils, and the outer face of the Double Dentil, very nearly, Fig. 90.

(*b*)   Where they cut the lower line of the Modillion Band:

17.   The width of the Modillion, and the outer face of the Modillion Band, Fig. 90.

(The distance from the edge of the Corona down to the lower edge of the Modillion Band is one-third the distance down to the top of the Frieze, and the distance down to the lower edge of the Ovolo, one-half.)

THE IONIC VOLUTE

The vertical line *a b*, Fig. 91, through the center of the eye of the Ionic Volute, and the horizontal line *c d*, will mark in the circumference of the eye the four corners of a square within which a fret may be drawn whose angles will serve as centers, from which the curves of the volute may be described mechanically.   The sides of the square above referred to should be bisected, and through the upper points thus located a horizontal line *e f* should be drawn.   Now, with *e g* as a radius, the arc *g f* may be drawn as the first section of the volute.   Now, through the point *h*, where the line *e f* bisects the side of the square, a vertical line *h k* should be drawn, and with *h f* as a radius the arc *f k* may be struck.   From *h* and *e* lines should be drawn at 45 degrees, intersecting at the center of the eye, and the line extending from *h* to the center should be divided into three equal parts, through which the corners of the inscribed fret will turn. The point *l* on the line *h k*, marking the lower left-hand corner of the inscribed fret, is located five-sixths of the distance between *h* and the point where *h k* bisects the lower side of the square. *l* then forms the center for the arc *k m*, and the rest of the volute is described from centers found at the angles of the inscribed fret.

VERTICAL LINES

The outer line of the upper Diameter of the Shaft gives, in all the Orders, Figs. 84 and 85:

18. The face of the lower band of the Architrave, and
19. The face of the Frieze.

In the Denticulated Doric, it gives, Fig. 85:

20. The outer face of the first Dentil, next the Double Dentil.

FIG. 92. Doric

In the Ionic and Corinthian Orders, it gives, Figs. 84 and 85:

21. The axis of the first Interdentil.

The outer line of the lower Diameter of the Shaft, produced upwards, gives, Figs. 84 and 85:

22. The projection of the Astragal, in all the Orders, except the Tuscan and Doric.

23. The projection of the Tænia in the Tuscan and Doric.

24. The projection of the Fillet, in the Bed Mold of the Mutulary Doric, Fig. 85.

FIG. 93. Ionic

25. Twice the projection of the Triglyph, which is seen in profile.

26. Half the projection of the Tuscan Bed Mold, of the Tuscan and Doric Abacus, and of the Doric Mutule Band.

It also gives:

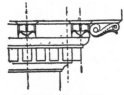

FIG. 94. Corinthian

27. The Axis of the Extreme Dentil, or first half of the Double Dentil, in the Denticulated Doric, Ionic, Corinthian, and Composite Orders, Figs. 92, 93, 94, and 95.

28. The position of the Eye of the Ionic Scroll, which is on a level with the bottom of the Echinus, Fig. 91.

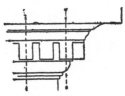

FIG. 95. Composite

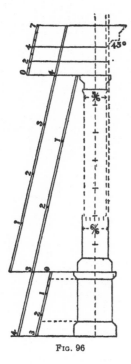

FIG. 96

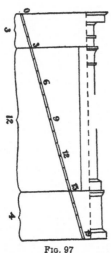

FIG. 97

DRAWING

General Proportions.—Since the relative size of all the parts, in Vignola's Orders, is fixed, any of them can be drawn out in accordance with these rules, if a single dimension is determined. The width of a Dentil or the length of a Modillion suffices to determine everything else. But the data generally given are either the lower Diameter of a Column, the height of a Column, or the whole height of the Order, with or without a Pedestal.

I. If the lower Diameter is given, the procedure is as follows, Fig. 96: Divide it in two, draw the axis of the Column, and then divide each half into three equal parts, Fig. 109; this gives the scale of sixths. Divide in two the two outer sixths; this gives the upper Diameter of the shaft, which is five-sixths. Lay off on the axis the height of the Column—by Diameters, 7, 8, 9, or 10—and of the Entablature, which is one-fourth the height of the Column. Mark the height of the Base, half a Diameter, or three-sixths, and then that of the Capital, two-, three-, or seven-sixths.

Then divide the total height of the Entablature into seven, eight, eighteen, or ten equal parts, according as it is Tuscan, Doric, Ionic, or Corinthian, or use halves, quarters, or eighths of a Diameter, and mark the heights of the Architrave, Frieze, and Cornice, drawing horizontal lines through the points of division. (Fig. 96 illustrates this procedure for the Tuscan Order.) Then carry up, vertically, the outer lines of both the upper and the lower Diameters of the Shaft, drawing from the point where the line of the upper Diameter cuts the lower edge of the Cornice a line at 45 degrees to determine the projection of the Cymatium, or that of the Mutule or of the Corona.

Add one-third of the height of the Column for the Pedestal. Divide this into three equal parts, taking the upper third of the upper third for the Cap, and the lower two-thirds of the lower third for the Base. Vignola makes the Base of the Pedestal only one-ninth of the height of the Pedestal instead of two-ninths as here determined.

II. If the height of the Column is given, a fourth part of this added at the top gives the height of the Entablature, and a third part added below gives the height of the Pedestal, Fig. 96. One seventh, eighth, ninth, or tenth of the height of the Column gives the lower Diameter of the Shaft. The drawing may then be carried forwards as above.

III. If the total height of the Order is given, without the Pedestal, a division into five equal parts gives four parts for the Column and one for the Entablature, Fig. 96.

If there is a Pedestal, and it is of the regular height of one-third the height of the Column, the division of the total height must be into nineteen equal parts, four of which go to the Pedestal, twelve to the Column, and three to the Entablature, Fig. 97.

The lower Diameter can then be obtained from the height of the Column, and the drawing completed, as above.

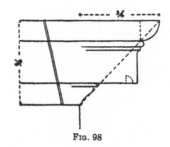

FIG. 98

NOTE.—The division of a given dimension into equal parts may be effected with the dividers, or, more easily, by using a scale of equal parts that are the same in number as the desired subdivisions, but a little larger, and holding this scale obliquely between the extreme limits of the space to be divided, Figs. 96 and 97. The division of vertical dimensions into five, seven, eight, nine, ten, eighteen, or nineteen equal parts, as here required, is thus easily accomplished. To insure accuracy, the lines marking these divisions should be horizontal, not normal to the direction of the scale.

Cornices.—The Tuscan Cornice may be drawn by dividing its height into quarters, as is done in the figure, giving the upper quarter to the Ovolo and the lower to the bed mold, and the middle half to the Corona, Bead, and Fillet, Fig. 98. A 45-degree line gives the projection of the Bed Mold, Ovolo, and the Cornice itself.

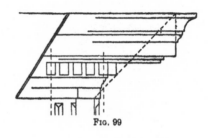

FIG. 99

The Doric Cornice is also divided into four equal parts, the upper one comprising the Cymatium and Fillet, the next the Corona and the small Cyma Reversa above it, the third the Mutules (or the Dentils with the Mutules above them), and the lower one the Bed Mold, including the Cap of the Triglyph, which is narrower in the Mutulary Doric than in the Denticulated by the width of the Fillet above it, Figs. 99 and 100.

A 45-degree line drawn outwards from the middle of the top of the Abacus gives, where it cuts the lower line of the Frieze, the projection of the Tænia. A similar line, where it cuts the upper line of the Frieze, gives the axes of the next Triglyph, Fig. 85. The Triglyphs are drawn next, with their Cap, and the Regula and Guttæ, then the Mutules, or the Dentils.

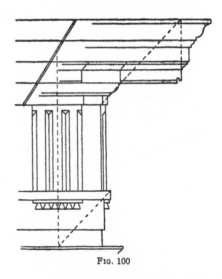

FIG. 100

In the Doric Order a line at 45 degrees drawn from the bottom of the Cornice gives the face of the Corona in the Denticulated Doric, the face of the Mutule in the Mutulary; in the other Orders, a similar line gives the projection of the Cymatium, Figs. 99 and 100.

In putting in Dentils, draw first the one over the Axis of the Column, then the Double Dentil, the first half of which is centered over the lower face of the Column, and then the intermediate ones, three, two, or one, according as the Order is Doric, Ionic, Corinthian, or Composite, Figs. 92, 93, 94, and 95. The Interdentil is half the width of the Dentil.

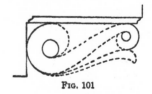

FIG. 101

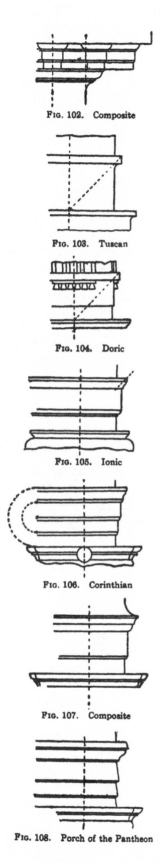

FIG. 102. Composite

FIG. 103. Tuscan

FIG. 104. Doric

FIG. 105. Ionic

FIG. 106. Corinthian

FIG. 107. Composite

FIG. 108. Porch of the Pantheon

One Corinthian Modillion comes over the axis of the corner column and one over the outer face of the Double Dentil, Fig. 94. In drawing the side of a Modillion, put in first, at the outer end, a semicircle half its height and one at the inner end nearly the whole height; then the rosettes, one twice as large as the other; then the connecting curves, and finally the leaf beneath, Fig. 101.

In Palladio's Composite Cornice, one block is set over the axis of the column, and the double block at the corner has its inner face on a line with the face of the Frieze below. The blocks are about half a Diameter, on centers, the inter-block being one twenty-fourth of a Diameter wider than the block itself, Fig. 102.

Architraves.—The Tuscan Architrave, Fig. 103, has but one fascia or band, the Composite two, Fig. 107, and the Corinthian three, Fig. 106. The Doric has sometimes one, but generally two, Fig. 104, and the Ionic has generally two, Fig. 105, but sometimes three. The lower band is always the narrowest and is set on a line with the face of the Shaft below and of the Frieze above.

All the Architraves have a Cymatium, or crowning member, which in the Tuscan and Doric is a broad Fillet, called the Tænia, and in the Ionic and Corinthian is a large Cyma Reversa, surmounted by a Fillet and generally supported by a bead. The lower bands often have, as a Cymatium, a small Cyma Reversa, Bead, or Ovolo, and all three bands are sometimes sloped backwards, as in the Entablature of the porch of the Pantheon in Rome, Fig. 108, so as to diminish the projection of the crowning moldings, which generally have a projection, beyond the face of the Frieze, equal to their height.

The Tuscan Tænia has beneath it the characteristic Tuscan congé, Fig. 103. Beneath the Doric Tænia, and directly under each Triglyph, Fig. 104, is a narrow Fillet, which sometimes has a beveled face, called the Regula, beneath which are the six Guttæ. These are sometimes frustra of cones, as in the Greek Order, sometimes of pyramids. The Guttæ, which almost touch at the bottom, are twice as high as the Regula. Both together are just as high as the Tænia, or one-twelfth of a Diameter, so that the three are one-sixth of a Diameter high. They accordingly occupy the upper third of the height of the Architrave, which is three-sixths high, the lower band occupying the lower third.

The two lower bands of the Corinthian Architrave occupy half its height, and the lower band with its Cymatium is just as wide as the moldings that crown the upper band. The second band with its Cymatium is just as wide as the third band without its Cymatium, Fig. 106.

Capitals and Bases.—In drawing Capitals, it is best to put in first the axis of the column and the vertical faces of the Shaft; then the horizontal lines, and lastly the profile, beginning at the top. But in drawing Bases, it is best to put in the profile of the molding before the horizontal lines.

The Tuscan Base, Fig. 109, is half a Diameter high, half of which goes to the Plinth and half to the Base Molding, which is made to include the Cincture, or broad Fillet at the bottom of the Shaft, which in the other Orders is not counted as part of the Base. But this is merely saying that the Tuscan Base is not quite half a Diameter high.

All the other Bases, including the Attic Base, are just half a Diameter high. All the Plinths are eight-sixths wide and one-sixth high, except the Tuscan and Doric, which are one-quarter of a Diameter high. It is not worth while to define the proportions of the other Bases.

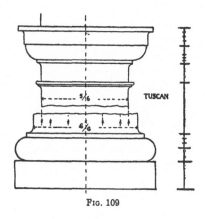

FIG. 109

The Tuscan Capital, Fig. 109, is half a Diameter high, or three-sixths, the upper sixth comprising the Abacus with its Fillet, the middle sixth the Echinus and the Fillet below it, and the lower sixth the Necking. The upper Fillet is a quarter of a sixth wide, the lower one a sixth of a sixth. The Abacus is seven-sixths wide; i. e., it projects one-sixth on each side beyond the upper diameter of the Shaft.

The Doric Capital, Fig. 110, is also three-sixths of a Diameter high, the two upper sixths being divided into thirds, and these again into thirds, to give the height of the smaller moldings. The Denticulated Capital generally has three Fillets, the Mutulary, a Bead and Fillet.

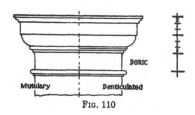

FIG. 110

The Astragal, which in the other Capitals is one-twelfth of a Diameter high, or half a sixth, is in the Tuscan and Doric Orders one-fourth smaller, or one-sixteenth of a Diameter, the Bead being one twenty-fourth of a Diameter high, or a quarter of a sixth. In drawing the Astragals, draw first the horizontal line at the top, which occupies two-thirds of the projection, otherwise the Congé below is apt to be slighted. The Bead and Congé should have their full measure of 180 degrees and 90 degrees, Fig. 111.

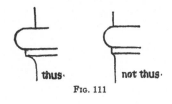

FIG. 111

The Ionic Capital, which is one-third of a Diameter in height, or four-twelfths, is also divided into three parts, but unequally. The Abacus occupies the upper quarter, or one-twelfth, and had better be put in first. The Echinus occupies rather more than half of the remaining space, namely, five-ninths. In the Composite Capital, the Abacus occupies the upper sixth, and a little more, and the Echinus and the Astragal the next one, Fig. 82.

The Eyes of the Ionic Scroll come in line with the top of the Astragal and with the lower Diameter of the Column, and should be put in first, Fig. 112. The Scrolls make three complete turns and finally are tangent to the upper side of the eye. They can best be drawn by putting in first three semicircles on the outer side, and then three smaller ones on the inner side. In working on a small scale, two semicircles on each side suffice, or three on the outer side and two on the inner, as in the figures. But one is never enough. The Eyes of the Composite and of the Roman Ionic Capitals are set nearer together, Fig. 82.

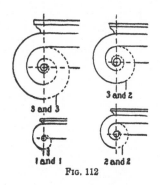

FIG. 112

In drawing a Corinthian Capital, Fig. 113, it is best to put

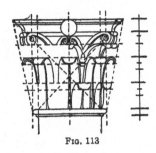

FIG. 113

FIG. 114

in first the Astragal and the lower line of the Architrave, carrying up on each side the outer lines of the Shaft; then the Abacus, Fleuron, and Scrolls. The double scroll at the corner falls just outside these vertical lines. It appears slightly elliptical in shape, not circular, and the outer scroll is more elliptical than the inner, being more foreshortened. The small scrolls under the Fleuron are also foreshortened into ellipses. Then the five leaves of second row, the middle one in elevation, the two side ones in profile, and the other two at 45 degrees, carrying down the mid-ribs to the Astragal. Their tips turn down half a sixth, those of the corner leaves coming just on the outer lines of the upper shaft. Of the four leaves of the lower row, the two inner ones occupy the spaces between these mid-ribs, and the ends that turn over fall entirely within the outline of the lower parts. The two outer leaves extend on either side slightly beyond the width of the shaft below, and their tips fall just outside the lower line of the leaves, being about six-sixths of a Diameter apart. They accordingly come just over the outer lines of the lower Diameter, just as the tips of the corner leaves above them come on the lines of the upper Diameter.

A line drawn tangent to the Astragal and to the Abacus is also tangent to all three rows of leaves, very nearly. The Caulicoli, the Buttons, the third row of leaves, and the lower parts of the Volutes follow, in this order.

The smaller the scale of the drawing, the more straight and upright should the Acanthus leaves be made, Fig. 114.

THE GREEK ORDERS

ALTHOUGH the different examples of the Greek Doric and
Ionic Orders differ considerably among themselves, both in
the proportions of the Columns and in the treatment of
details, the proportions of the Entablature are tolerably
uniform and are, in general, the same for both Orders, the
Architrave and Frieze being both about three-quarters of a
Diameter in height and the Cornice about half a Diameter,
Figs. 115 and 122. The Entablatures, as has been said, are
about two Diameters high, however tall or short the Columns
may be. Their chief characteristic is the height of the
Architrave and the shallowness of the Cornice. The Diminution and the Entasis of the Columns begin at the bottom of
the Shaft.

THE GREEK DORIC—PLATE XIV

The Greek Doric has no Base, the Shaft standing upon
three large steps, the upper one of which is called the *Stylobate*, Fig. 115. It has generally twenty Channels, Fig. 116,
which are generally elliptical in section, but some small
Columns have only sixteen, or even, as at Argos, fourteen,
Fig. 117. In a number of examples, an Arris instead of a
Channel comes on the axis of the Column, as is seen both at
Argos and at Assos, Fig. 118. Instead of an Astragal, a
groove, or *Sinkage*, separates the Shaft from the Necking
of the Capital, and the Channels are carried past it, through
the Necking, quite up to the Fillets at the base of the Echinus,
Fig. 116. These Fillets vary in number. They are not vertical on the face, but are parallel to the slope of the Echinus,
and their upper surfaces also are beveled, Fig. 119. The
Echinus itself has an elliptical or hyperbolic profile, the
earlier examples being the most convex and the later ones
hardly differing from a straight line. The Abacus has no
moldings.

The Architrave also is plain, and is crowned by a Tænia,
below which is a broad Regula and six short Guttæ. In the
earlier examples, the face of the Architrave is set just over
and in line with the upper Diameter of the Shaft, but in the
later ones it overhangs, coming over the lower Diameter, and
the Echinus is made steeper, as well as straighter, as has been
said, as if to support it.

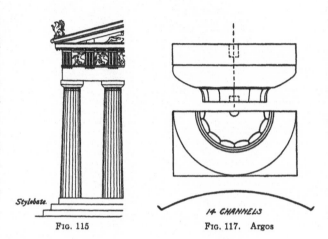

Stylobate.

FIG. 115

FIG. 117. Argos

14 CHANNELS

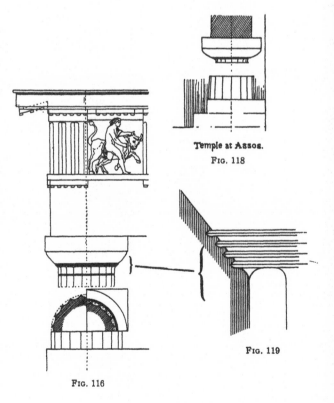

Temple at Assos.
FIG. 118

FIG. 119

FIG. 116

FIG. 120

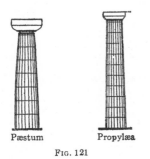

Pæstum   Propylæa

FIG. 121

The Triglyphs in the Frieze are shorter and broader than in the Roman Doric, and are set flush with the Architrave below, the Metopes being set back. They are also thicker than those in the Roman Orders, and the channels are much larger, being one-fourth wider,—measuring two-ninths, or four-eighteenths, of the width of the Triglyph instead of one-sixth, or three-eighteenths,—and also deeper. The half channels on the edges go back at an angle of 45 degrees, and the two whole channels generally at 60 degrees, the cross-section being thus an equilateral triangle cutting deeply into the face of the Triglyph; they run nearly up to the broad Fillet, or Band, that constitutes the Cap of the Triglyph. This is only as wide as the Triglyph itself, not breaking round the corners, and it is not continued between the Triglyphs, the Cap of the Metopes being narrower.

As in Vignola's Denticulated Doric, the Mutules on the Soffit of the Corona slope up, and have only eighteen Guttæ, and they occur over the Metopes as well as over the Triglyphs, Fig. 120. The Mutules are thicker than those in the Denticulated Doric, though not so thick as in the Mutulary. The Cymatium generally consists of an elliptical Ovolo and a Fillet, the Soffit of which is beveled. But different examples vary in almost every one of these particulars.

At the corner of a building the Triglyphs are set, not over the axis of the Column, but at the extreme end of the Frieze, two coming together and making a solid block. As the Metopes do not vary in size, being nearly square, this brings the three corner columns nearer together than the others.

In the best Greek examples the axes of the columns all slope in a little, so that the corner column, which is a little bigger than the others, has its inner face nearly vertical. The horizontal lines, both of the Entablature and of the Stylobate, curve slightly, being convex up, the vertical faces incline a little, either out or in, and the moldings are, as has been said, generally elliptical or hyperbolic in section, rather than arcs of circles.

The columns vary in height from about five to eight Diameters, the earlier ones being the shortest, and the Entasis, or Curvature in the outline of the Shaft, and the Diminution in the width of the Shaft, from bottom to top, which sometimes amounts to one-third of the Diameter, are much more pronounced in the earlier examples than in the later ones, Fig. 121. This seems to show that the original of the Doric column was not a wooden post, as has been thought, nor a pile of masonry, but was probably a piece of rubble work, covered, like the rubble walls, with stucco.

THE GREEK IONIC—PLATE XV

THE general proportions of the Greek Ionic Entablature are, as has been said, about the same as in the Doric, but the Columns are more slender, varying from about seven Diameters in height to more than ten, and the Architrave, Frieze, and Cornice are often made very nearly equal in height, Fig. 122.

The Base is like the Attic Base, except that the Scotia is larger, constituting the principal feature, that the upper Torus is larger than the lower one, that the Fillet above the Scotia projects as far as the face of this Torus, and that there is no Plinth. As the base is still half a Diameter high, the upper Torus and Scotia are very much larger than in the Roman Attic Base. The lower Torus is sometimes very small indeed, and is occasionally omitted altogether, as at Samos, Fig. 123, and in one of the Choragic columns on the south side of the Acropolis at Athens, Fig. 69.

The Shaft is fluted just as in the Roman Ionic, having twenty-four channels, and the Capital resembles, in general, Vignola's Capital with Balusters. But the Scrolls are much larger, measuring a full Diameter and a half from side to side, and two-thirds of a Diameter from the Architrave to the bottom of the curve. The Capital, measured from the Architrave down to the Astragal, is half a Diameter high, instead of a third, the Abacus is very small, consisting generally of a single Ovolo, and the *Cushion* between the Abacus and the Echinus very wide, its lower outline being curved downwards, Fig. 124. The sprigs of honeysuckle, accordingly, do not cover the eggs and darts, five of which are visible between the Scrolls, instead of three.

The Architrave is sometimes plain, sometimes divided into two or three bands. The Frieze, or Zoöphorus, is wide, and the Bed Mold that crowns it is often countersunk into the Soffit of the Corona, so that it does not show in elevation, Fig. 122. It is noticeable that though Dentils are, historically, a distinctively Ionic feature, they are omitted in many Greek examples. The Cymatium is a large Cyma Recta, and has a Fillet and Bead below it, which is sometimes undercut, so as to make a little Beak Molding.

FIG. 122

FIG. 123

FIG. 124

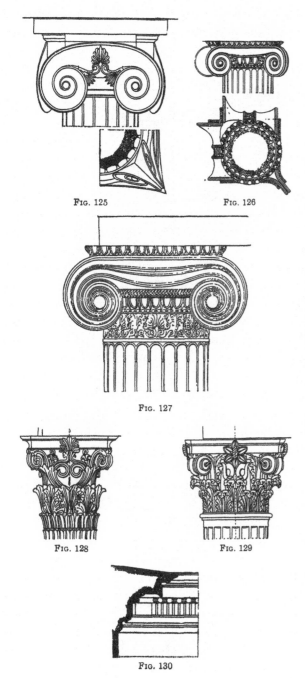

FIG. 125   FIG. 126

FIG. 127

FIG. 128   FIG. 129

FIG. 130

But here, as in the Greek Doric, there is a great variety in the details of different buildings.

The four faces of the Capital are sometimes made alike, with double Scrolls on each corner, as in the Roman Ionic, and these Scrolls are sometimes connected under the Abacus by a continuous curve, convex up, instead of by a horizontal line, Fig. 125. Sometimes a corner column shows Scrolls on the two outer faces and Balusters on the two inner ones, the double scroll on the corner projecting at 45 degrees, Fig. 126. Some examples have a wide Necking, adorned with the honeysuckle ornament, below the Echinus, Fig. 127.

A few Corinthian Capitals are to be found in Greece, but the buildings in which they occur are in other respects Ionic, or even Doric, Fig. 128.

In the later Greek colonies in Southern Italy are found interesting varieties of all the Orders.

Their most marked peculiarity is the treatment of the details, Fig. 130. The Triglyphs and Dentils are long and slender, and the moldings refined in outline and sometimes separated by deep grooves, rectangular or circular, which are not to be mistaken for moldings. The Architraves lose their importance, the Ionic Scrolls are often diminished in size, and the egg-and-dart molding is changed into what are sometimes called *Filberts*, Fig. 131. The Corinthian Capitals receive a local development quite unlike that which was finally adopted in Rome itself, as may be witnessed at Tivoli, Fig. 129, Pompeii, and Herculaneum, Fig. 132. Since the revival of classical architecture other variations have appeared in France, Germany, and Italy.

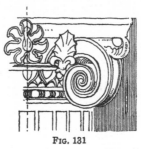

FIG. 131

FIG. 132

PILASTERS—PLATE XVI

THE Romans made their Pilaster Capitals resemble those of the Columns. This works well, except with the Ionic Capital, in which the projecting Echinus presents an almost insuperable difficulty, Fig. 133.

As Pilasters do not generally diminish in width at the top, their Capitals are one-fifth broader than those of the Columns. In this case the Architrave comes in line with the upper face of the column, and the face of the Pilaster projects one-twelfth Diameter beyond it, as appears in the perpectives given in Plates III, IV, VIII, X, and XII. But Pilasters are often made half a sixth narrower than the Columns at the bottom, and half a sixth wider at the top, having thus a uniform Diameter of five-sixths and a half. In the Corinthian Pilaster Capital, the extra space is taken up by making the leaves a little broader, and setting them farther apart, Fig. 134.

Pilasters generally project from the wall a quarter of their diameter, but sometimes have to be made thicker in order to receive string-courses or other horizontal moldings that they cut across. If made much thicker than this, they are apt to look thicker than the columns alongside them, and piers always do, noticeably enhancing the slenderness of the columns near them.

The Greeks gave their Pilasters Bases like those of the Columns, but Capitals of their own, composed of a series of moldings, Fig. 135.

Pilasters are preferable to half columns, which always look smaller than they are, and have a mean appearance. Moreover, any moldings that they interrupt seem to cut them in two, Fig. 136. In these respects, three-quarter columns are better, though they are apt to look clumsy, and they inevitably make an awkward junction with the wall behind them. They also make it uncertain which is the principal supporting member, the wall or the column.

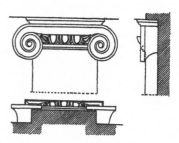

FIG. 133

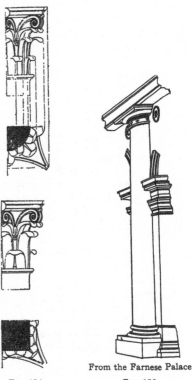

From the Farnese Palace

FIG. 136

FIG. 134

FIG. 135

PEDESTALS—PLATE XVI

As has already been said, a short Pier is called a Post, and, if it supports something, a Pedestal, and the Pedestals that support Columns are generally made one-third the height of the Column. The Cap is one-ninth the height of the Pedestal, and generally consists of a Bed Mold and Corona. There is no Cymatium, a gutter being obviously out of place, but the Corona is crowned by a fillet and small Cyma Reversa. The Base, which is two-ninths of the height of the Pedestal, or, according to Vignola, only one-ninth, like the Cap, consists of a Plinth and Base Moldings, among which a Cyma Recta is generally conspicuous, with a Torus below it.

The moldings, in both Cap and Base, are fewer and consequently larger and simpler in the Tuscan and Doric Orders than in the Ionic and Corinthian, the Tuscan, according to Vignola, having no Corona, and the Corinthian a Necking and Astragal. The Cap projects less than its own height, in many examples, and the Plinth just as much as the Corona.

But Pedestals vary greatly both in their proportions and in their moldings.

PARAPETS

A wall low enough to lean upon is called a *Parapet*, and whether low or high is often strengthened by occasional Posts or Pedestals, sometimes of the same height, sometimes higher. In either case the wall or parapet has a Cap and Base, which may or may not be like those of the Pedestals or Posts. A similar strip of wall, with the wall continued above the Cap, is called a *Continuous Pedestal*, Fig. 143. This often occurs between the Pedestals that support Pilasters.

BALUSTRADES

In antiquity, Parapets were often pierced by triangular penetrations, apparently in imitation of wooden fences, Fig. 137. But in modern times the openings in Parapets are generally filled with a sort of colonnade of dwarfed columns called *Balusters*. These frequently occupy the whole space between one Post or Pedestal and the next, forming a *Balustrade*, Fig. 138. If the distance is great, so that the Cap has to be made of several lengths of stone, a block called an *Uncut Baluster* is placed under the joint. Not more than a dozen Balusters should occur together without such interruption. Against the Pedestal is often set a *Half-Baluster*, or, which is better, half of an Uncut Baluster, to support the end of the Upper Rail, Fig. 139.

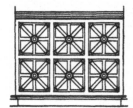

FIG. 137

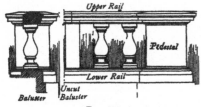

Upper Rail

Pedestal

Lower Rail

Baluster *Uncut Baluster*

FIG. 138

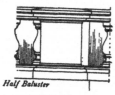

Half Baluster

FIG. 139

The Cap and Base of the Pedestals, or of the Parapet or Continuous Pedestal, are called in a Balustrade the *Upper* and *Lower Rails*. The Baluster supports the Upper Rail as a Column supports an Entablature, and stands upon the Lower Rail as upon a Stylobate, Fig. 139. It has its own Cap, the height of which, including the Astragal, is one-quarter the height of the Baluster, and which consists of a plain Abacus, Echinus and Fillet, and Necking. These three members are of equal height, as in the Tuscan and Doric Capitals.

The Base of the Baluster is also one-quarter its total height and resembles the Attic Base. The Scotia, as in the Greek Attic Base, is generally made the principal member.

Between the Cap and Base is the Shaft, or *Sleeve*, which has the outline of a Quirked Cyma Reversa, the greatest diameter, or *Belly*, coming at about one-fourth of its height, or one-third the height of the Baluster, Fig. 140. Its width at this point is also one-third the height of the Baluster, as is also that of the Plinth of the Base, exactly, and the width of the Abacus, almost. The Necking is less than half as wide. The point of contrary flexure in the Cyma Reversa is half way between Cap and Base, or between the Upper and Lower Rails. But these proportions are made somewhat lighter for use with the Ionic and Corinthian Orders.

The Rails are sometimes, in height, one-sixth and two-sixths of the space between them, like the Cap and Base of a Continuous Pedestal; but they are often made much heavier, even one-third and one-half.

Instead of the Cyma Reversa, a Beak Molding is often used, Fig. 141, and other variations are frequent. Of these, the most important is the so-called *Double Baluster*, which consists of two small Balusters, set together base to base just like the Baluster on the side of an Ionic Capital, Fig. 142. Vignola also used a high block under the Plinth. Balusters are often made square in section, like piers, instead of round, like columns.

Balusters are set about half their height apart, on centers.

A Balustrade, like a Parapet, is intended to lean upon, and should not be more than 3 or 4 feet high. While, therefore, Columns and Entablatures are proportioned to the size of the buildings in which they occur, varying in height from 10 or 12 feet to 50 or 60, Balustrades, like steps, are proportioned to the size of the human figure, and in large buildings are relatively much smaller than in small ones. They thus serve, as do steps, and as does the human figure when introduced into a drawing, to indicate the scale of a building.

But in very large buildings Balustrades have sometimes been made of colossal dimensions, that on the top of the front of St. Peter's, for example, being about 8 feet high.

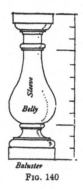

Baluster
FIG. 140

FIG. 141

FIG. 142

ATTICS

WHEN a Parapet is placed on top of an Entablature it is called an *Attic*, that is to say, an "Athenian" story, Fig. 143. Like Pedestals, Attics vary much in size and in architectural treatment. They are generally made about a quarter as high as the Order below, and should not be more than a third, and they should have a high Plinth, or even a double Plinth, Figs. 144 and 153, so as not to be too much hidden by the projection of the Cornices on which they stand.

The place of an Attic is often taken by Balustrades, Fig. 145. which also should have high Plinths, below the lower rail.

FIG. 143   FIG. 144

FIG. 145

PEDIMENTS—PLATE XVII

THE Gable upon a Classical building is called a *Pediment*, Fig. 146. It consists of a Triangular piece of wall, called the *Tympanum*, which is in the same plane as the Frieze below; of a *Horizontal Cornice*, which divides the Tympanum from the Frieze; and of two pieces of inclined cornice that surmount the Tympanum. The inclined, or *Raking*, *Cornice* is like the cornice that crowns the wall on the sides of the building, but the Cymatium is a little wider. The Horizontal Cornice has no Cymatium, and generally terminates in a Fillet, called the *Split Fillet*, which divides at the angle where the two Cornices come together.

If the Cymatium is a Cavetto, the under side of the Fillet beneath it is beveled, either on the rake or along the wall; if it is an Ovolo, the same thing happens to the Fillet above it, Fig. 147. With the Cyma Reversa both occur, with the Cyma Recta, neither, the fillets having no soffit. This is one of the reasons for employing this molding in this place.

When a Cyma Recta is used in the Cymatium, it occurs in four different forms, Fig. 148; viz.: (1) the profile of the molding along the wall; (2) the profile of the raking molding; (3) the line of intersection of these two moldings—this lies in a vertical plane, set at 45 degrees; (4) the line of intersection of the two raking moldings at the top. (1), (2), and (4) have the same projection but different heights; (1) and (3) have the same height but not the same projection.

According to Vignola, the obtuse angle at the top of the Pediment is included within an arc of 90 degrees. It accordingly gives a slope of 22½ degrees. This is a good rule for most cases. But if a building is high and narrow, the slope needs to be steeper, and if it is low and wide, flatter. Inasmuch, however, as, for a building of a given width, the higher it is, the larger is the scale of the Order employed and of all the details of the Order, it follows that, for a given width of front, the larger the moldings are, the steeper must be the slope.

FIG. 146

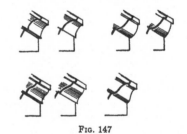

FIG. 147

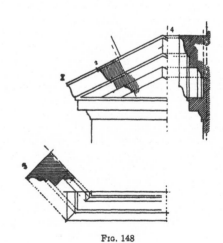

FIG. 148

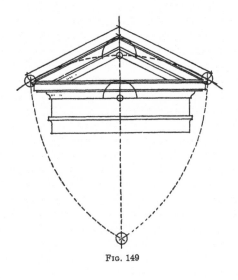

FIG. 149

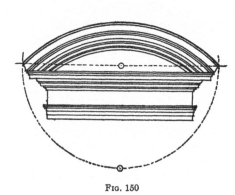

FIG. 150

Upon this is founded the following rule for the slope of Pediments, devised by Stanislas L'Eveillé, Fig. 149: Taking the upper line of the Horizontal Cornice as one side, construct below it an equilateral triangle, and taking the vertex of this triangle as a center, and its side as a radius, describe an arc of 60 degrees. Taking, then, the summit of this arc as a center, describe a circle, the radius of which is equal to the width of the horizontal cornice. Lines drawn from the extremities of the Corona tangent to this circle will give the upper line of the Raking Corona. It is obvious that the larger the cornice, relatively to the length of the front, the steeper will be the slope. It is also plain that this rule gives steeper Pediments for the Corinthian and Ionic Orders than for the Doric and Tuscan, and for the Roman Orders than for the Greek, the cornices being wider.

Circular, or *Curved*, *Pediments* have a sweep of 90 degrees, Fig. 150, starting at an angle of 45 degrees.

When Pediments are used merely for ornament the upper part is sometimes omitted, giving a *Broken Pediment*, Fig. 152.

If the molding that crowns the Corona is omitted, the faces of the three Coronas are continuous, Fig. 151. This was exemplified in Antiquity by the recently discovered Treasury of the Cnidians at Delphi.

FIG. 151

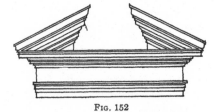

FIG. 152

INTERCOLUMNIATION, OR THE SPACING OF COLUMNS—PLATE XVIII

THE space between two columns, measured just above their bases, is called an *Intercolumniation*. It is one Diameter less than their distance apart on centers, or on edges.

Columns are said to be *Coupled*, or to have a *Pycnostyle, Systyle, Diastyle*, or *Areostyle Intercolumniation*, according as they are set close together, or are one, two, three, or four Diameters apart, as nearly as may be; i. e., about one, two, three, four, or five Diameters on centers. The Systyle and Diastyle are the most usual, with an Intercolumniation of two or of three Diameters.

But Coupled Columns cannot be nearer than one and one-third Diameters, on centers, instead of one Diameter, on account of the projection of their bases, and in the Ionic, Corinthian, and Composite Orders, not nearer than one and one-half Diameters, on account of the projection of their Capitals. The Intercolumniation of Coupled Columns is accordingly one-third or one-half of a Diameter, or even a little more, to prevent the Bases or Caps from actually touching. As this brings them eight-sixths Diameters, or nine-sixths Diameters,

FIG. 153

on centers, the Ionic and Corinthian dentils, which are one-sixth Diameter on centers occur exactly on the axis of the columns. This occurs also with the dentils of Vignola's Composite Order, which are one-fourth Diameter on centers, since nine-sixths Diameters equals six-fourths Diameters, and there is just room for five dentils over the Intercolumniation. But since the Corinthian Modillions are four-sixths Diameters on centers, and the shafts of Coupled Columns are nine-sixths Diameters on centers, it is necessary to widen each of the two caissons between the Modillions by one-twelfth Diameter, and increase the width of the Dentils and Interdentils by one-eighth, making the Dentils one-eighth Diameter in width instead of one-ninth Diameter, and the Interdentils one-sixteenth Diameter instead of one-eighteenth Diameter. [$\frac{1}{9} \times 1\frac{1}{8} = \frac{1}{8}$; $\frac{1}{18} \times 1\frac{1}{8} = \frac{1}{16}$.]

So also the Pycnostyle Intercolumniation is made one and one-fourth Diameters instead of one Diameter (i. e., two and one-fourth Diameters on centers, instead of two) to avoid crowding. The ancients thought that even the Systyle columns, with an Intercolumniation of two Diameters, came too near together, and preferred what they called the *Eustyle Intercolumniation*, of two and one-half Diameters (or three and one-half Diameters on centers, in place of three Diameters). But the moderns prefer to make the Eustyle Intercolumniation two and one-third Diameters (setting the columns three and one-third Diameters, on centers), as this brings every Column in Ionic and Corinthian colonnades exactly under a Dentil, and every alternate one just under a Modillion, the Dentils being one-sixth of a Diameter on centers, and the Modillions two-thirds of a Diameter.

The wider Intercolumniations are preferable, obviously, when the columns are small, since otherwise it might be difficult to get between them, and the Systyle, or even the Pycnostyle, when the columns are very large, since otherwise it might be difficult to find stone architraves long enough to span the interval. But the ancients used Tuscan Columns chiefly with wooden architraves, setting them as much as seven Diameters apart, which is called the *Tuscan Intercolumniation*, and which makes the space between the columns about square. In modern times, also, an arrangement of coupled columns has been employed, called *Areosystyle*, the columns being set half a Diameter apart, and the space between the pairs of columns made three and one-half Diameters. This is greater than the Diastyle Intercolumniation and less than the Areostyle by half a Diameter. From the axis of one pair of columns to that of the next pair the distance is six Diameters. If in a Systyle Colonnade, with the columns three Diameters on centers, the alternate columns are moved along until they nearly touch the intervening ones, the result is an Areostyle Colonnade. This was first used by Perrault in the Eastern Colonnade of the Louvre, Fig. 153.

In actual practice these rules for Intercolumniation are seldom exactly followed.

DORIC INTERCOLUMNIATIONS—PLATE XVIII

In the Doric Order, since the Columns come exactly under the Triglyphs and the Triglyphs are one and one-fourth Diameters on centers, as on edges (the width of the Triglyph being one-half of a Diameter and that of the Metopes three-fourths of a Diameter), the distance of the Columns on centers must needs be a multiple of one and one-fourth Diameters.

This makes the coupling of Doric Columns difficult, since, even if the Bases touch, the distance between axes is still one and one-third Diameters, which is more than that of the Triglyphs by one-twelfth of a Diameter. This slight discrepancy can, however, be got over by making each Base a trifle narrower, or the Triglyphs and Metopes a trifle wider, or by putting the Columns *not* exactly under the Triglyphs, or by employing all these devices at once.

If the Columns are set under alternate Triglyphs so that there is one Triglyph over the intervening space, their distance apart on centers is two and one-half Diameters. The Intercolumniation is then one and one-half Diameters, and is said to be *Monotriglyph*. This is the most common arrangement. But if the scale is small, it is usual, at least at the principal entrance of a building, to have two Triglyphs over the opening, the Columns being three and three-fourths Diameters on centers. The Intercolumniation is then two and three-fourths Diameters, and is called *Ditriglyph*. Still wider spacing is employed when the Architraves are of wood.

When two, four, six, eight, ten, or twelve Columns are used in a Colonnade or Portico, it is said to be *Distyle*, *Tetrastyle*, *Hexastyle*, *Octastyle*, *Decastyle*, or *Dodecastyle*, according to the Greek numerals. Examples are found at Argos, Assos, Thoricus, and Pæstum of façades with an odd number of columns, three, five, seven, and nine, a column instead of an intercolumniation coming on the axis, giving *tristyle*, *pentastyle*, *heptastyle*, and *enneastyle* porticos. But in all these cases the entrances were apparently on the sides of the buildings, where there was an even number of columns.

SUPERPOSITION—PLATE XVIII

SUPERPOSITION is the placing of one Order above another, as in the Roman Amphitheaters and in many modern buildings of several stories. The more solid forms of the Tuscan and Doric are naturally placed below, and the Ionic and Corinthian above. The Composite is sometimes placed below the Corinthian, as being more vigorous. But in high buildings it is generally placed on the top story, its large details being better seen at a distance than are those of the more delicate Order.

Even when the same Order is employed in the different stories it is advisable to have the upper Columns of smaller diameter than those below, and all the dimensions diminished accordingly, for the sake of lightness. But it is still more so when different Orders are superposed, for otherwise the Doric and Corinthian stories would overpower the Tuscan and Ionic ones beneath (Plate XVIII, A). It is usual, accordingly, to make the lower diameter of each Shaft equal to the upper diameter of the Shaft below it, as if they were all cut from a single piece of tapering stone (Plate XVIII, B). This makes the scale employed in the second story five-sixths of that used in the first; in the third, twenty-five thirty-sixths, or about two-thirds; in the fourth, about three-fifths, and in the fifth, about one-half, if the Five Orders are employed in regular sequence; this makes the relative height of the Orders in the successive stories to be as 7, $6\frac{2}{3}$, $6\frac{1}{4}$, $5\frac{5}{8}$, and 5, very nearly. The actual height of the stories themselves may be somewhat modified by the use of plinths and pedestals.

This system of Superposition makes the distance apart of the Columns in each story, when expressed in terms of their own Diameter, six-fifths of that in the story below. A Eustyle Intercolumniation in one story thus exactly produces a Diastyle Intercolumniation in the story above, and a Doric Monotriglyph Intercolumniation, a Systyle (Plate XVIII, F).

$$(\tfrac{6}{5} \times 3\tfrac{1}{3} = 4;\ \tfrac{6}{5} \times 2\tfrac{1}{2} = 3)$$

Coupled Columns set one and one-third Diameters apart, on centers, in one story, are, in the story above, one and three-fifths Diameters o. c., and in the third story nearly two Diameters o. c. This does very well for

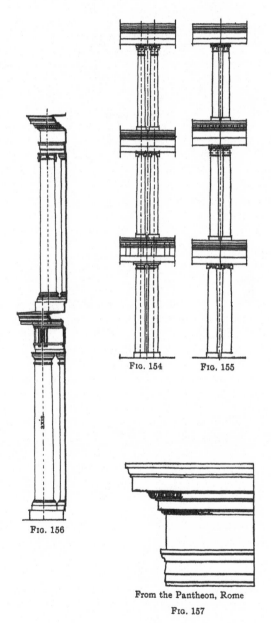

FIG. 154   FIG. 155

FIG. 156

From the Pantheon, Rome
FIG. 157

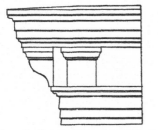

From the Fourth Order of the Collosseum

Fig. 158

From the Villa Caprarola. By Vignola

Fig. 159

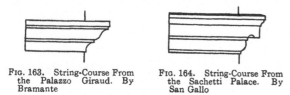

Fig. 160   Fig. 161
From the Farnese Palace
By San Gallo

Fig. 162. String-Course
From the Strozzi Palace

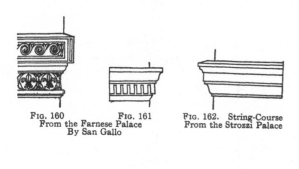

Fig. 163. String-Course From
the Palazzo Giraud. By
Bramante

Fig. 164. String-Course From
the Sachetti Palace. By
San Gallo

a sequence of Doric, Ionic, and Corinthian, Fig. 154. But if the lower Columns are Ionic or Corinthian those above had better be set nearer together, the axis of the Intercolumniation only being preserved, Fig. 155.

With this exception, Superposed Columns are set so that their axes are in the same vertical line, when seen in elevation. But in profile, as seen in section, the upper ones are set back, the wall against which they stand generally growing thinner as it goes up, Fig. 156. Since the Columns themselves also grow smaller, it would not do to leave too much space behind them. The slightly pyramidal effect that this gives to a building of several stories is of value, preventing it from looking top-heavy and high-shouldered (Plate XVIII, C).

OTHER CORNICES AND STRING-COURSES

The Five Orders worked out by Vignola are generally accepted as a standard, though they are seldom exactly followed in practice, modern as well as ancient examples exhibiting a great variety in the forms and proportions of the parts. But familiarity with them is of great service in designing, since they can safely be employed on all ordinary occasions, and in the earlier stages of architectural composition. Other types of nearly equal merit have been published by Alberti, Palladio, Serlio, Scamozzi, Sir William Chambers, and others, and a great variety of cornices, both with and without friezes and architraves, have been employed in ancient and modern times to crown and protect walls that were not decorated with columns or pilasters.

Many of these show Blocks or Modillions without any Dentil Course below, as on Palladio's Composite Cornice, and in many of them the Dentil Course is plain, forming what is called an *Uncut Dentil Course*, Fig. 157. In others, the brackets that support the Corona are brought down so as to occupy the Frieze, Fig. 158. The most important of these is Vignola's so-called *Cantilever Cornice* used by him at Caprarola, Fig. 159. It seems to have been suggested by the Mutules and Triglyphs of his Mutulary Doric.

Cornices, and indeed full Entablatures, are often used as String-Courses to separate stories, as in the Roman Amphitheaters. But it is customary to use, instead, a lighter form, of small projection, somewhat like the cap of a pedestal, in which the Cymatium and Bed Mold are often omitted, and the Corona itself sometimes diminished to a mere fillet, Figs. 160 to 164.

PART I
The Plates

PLATE 1

MOULDINGS

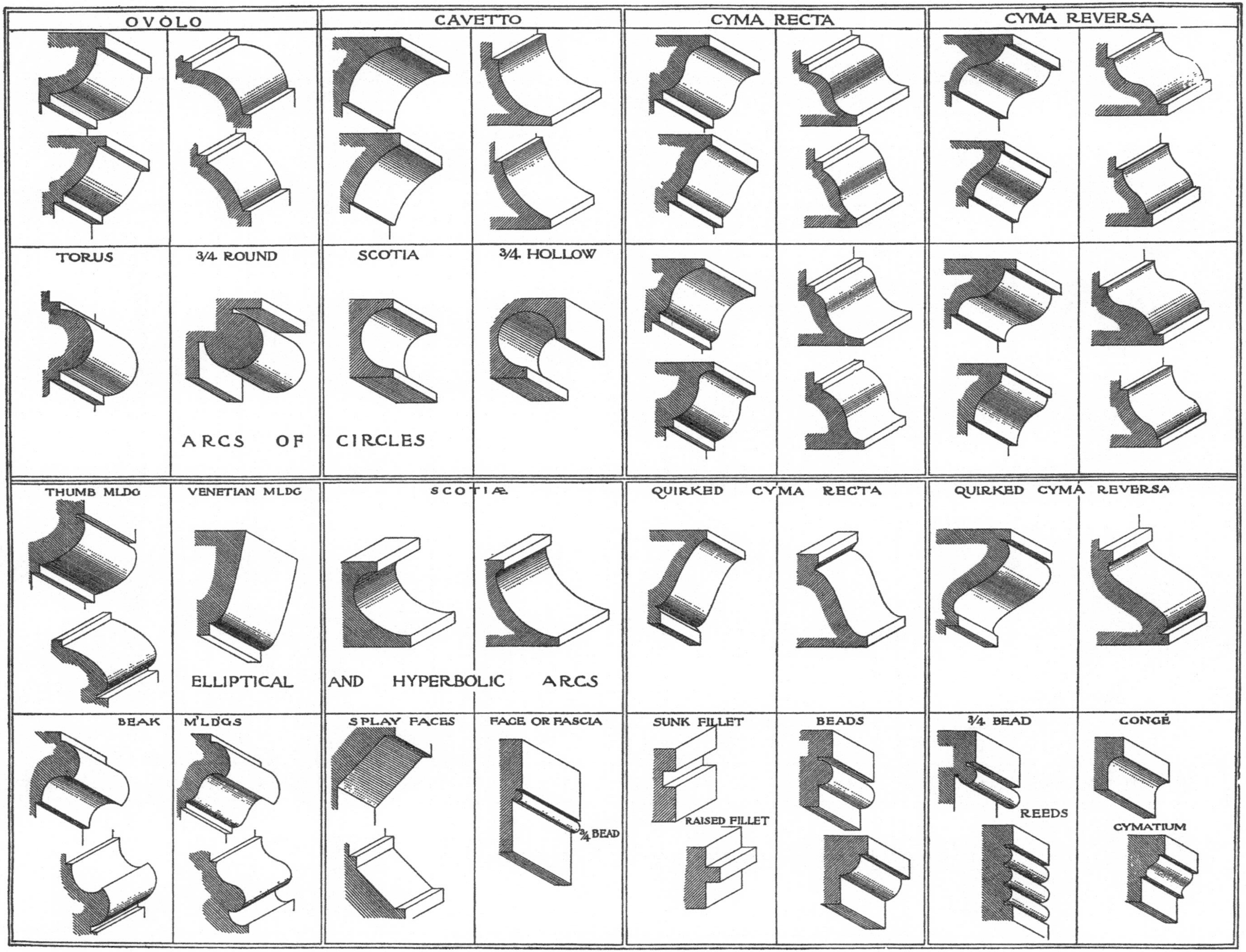

CYMA REVERSA

QUIRKED CYMA REVERSA

CONGÉ

CYMATIUM

3/4 BEAD

REEDS

CYMA RECTA

CYMA RECTA

BEADS

QUIRKED

SUNK FILLET

RAISED FILLET

CAVETTO

3/4 HOLLOW

SCOTIA

CIRCLES

SCOTIA

ARCS

FACE OR FASCIA

3/4 BEAD

AND HYPERBOLIC

SPLAY FACES

OVOLO

3/4 ROUND

ARCS OF

VENETIAN MLDG

ELLIPTICAL

M'LDGS

TORUS

THUMB MLDG

BEAK

COMPARISON OF THE ORDERS

PLATE II

TYPE OF ORDER	NAMES OF FEATURES		GREEK DORIC	TUSCAN	DORIC	IONIC	CORINTHIAN COMPOSITE	PERSPECTIVE VIEW
ENTABLATURE (1/4 to 1/5)	CORNICE	OVATIUM / CORONA / BED MOULD	1/2	3/4	3/4	7/8	1 — 3/4	
	FRIEZE	TÆNIA	2	1¾	2	2¼	2½	
	ARCHITRAVE		3/4	1/2	3/4	6/8	3/4	
			3/4	1/2	1/2	5/8	3/4	
COLUMN (1)	CAPITAL	ABACUS / ECHINUS / NECKING / ASTRAGAL	1/2	1/2	1/2	1/3 [1/2]	7/6	FROM WITHOUT
	SHAFT		4-6	7	8 7	9 8	10 8⅓	
	BASE	CINCTURE / BASE MOULD / PLINTH	NONE	1/2	1/2	1/2	1/2	FROM WITHIN
PEDESTAL (1/3 ≡)	CAP	CORONA / BED MOULDING	NO PEDESTAL BUT THREE STEPS THE STYLOBATE			1/3	THE CAP IS ONE NINTH THE HEIGHT OF THE PEDESTAL	
	DIE						PEDESTAL 1/3 [VIGNOLA]	
	BASE	BASE MOULD / PLINTH					THE BASE IS TWO NINTHS THE HEIGHT OF THE PEDESTAL	

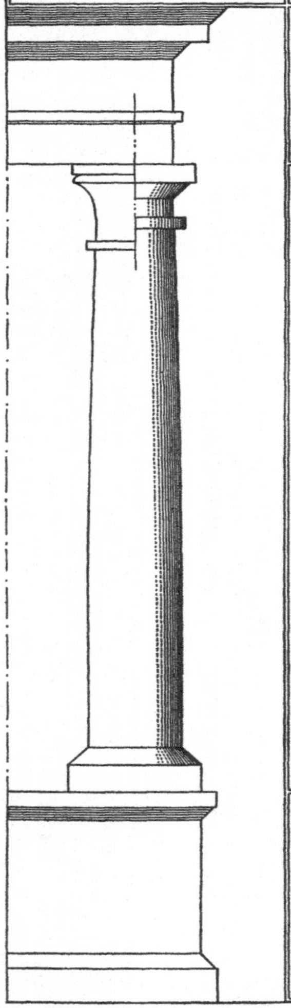

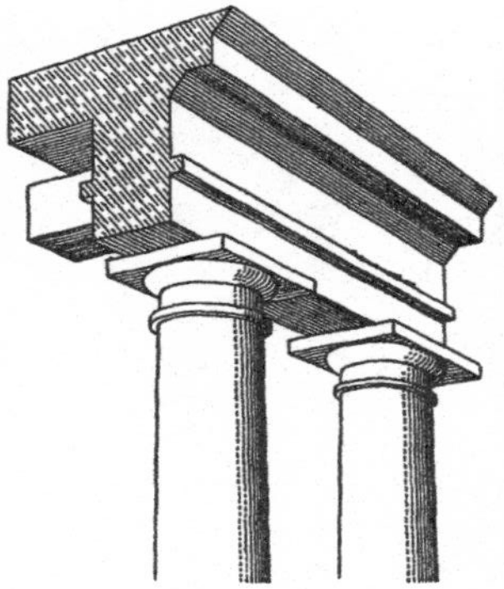

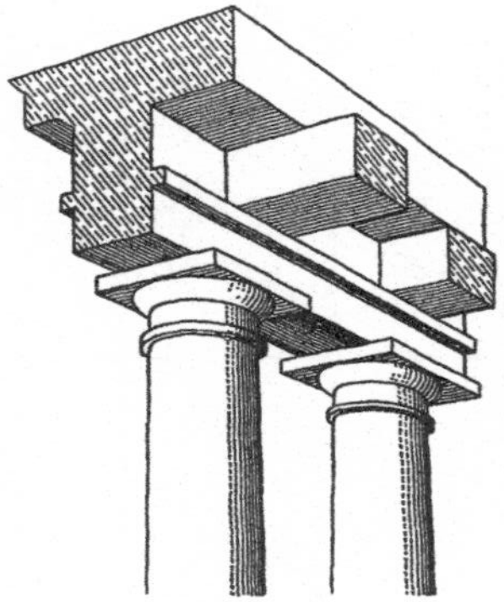

TUSCAN ORDER

PLATE III

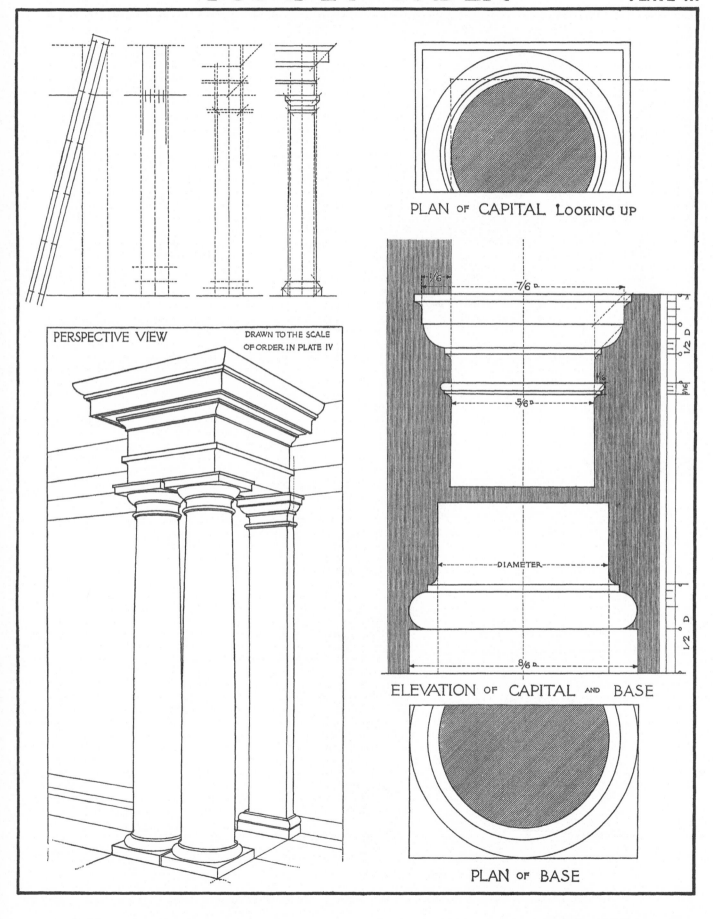

PLAN OF CAPITAL LOOKING UP

PERSPECTIVE VIEW

DRAWN TO THE SCALE OF ORDER IN PLATE IV

7/6 D.

5/6 D.

DIAMETER

8/6 D.

1/2 D

1/2 D

ELEVATION OF CAPITAL AND BASE

PLAN OF BASE

TUSCAN ORDER

PLATE IV

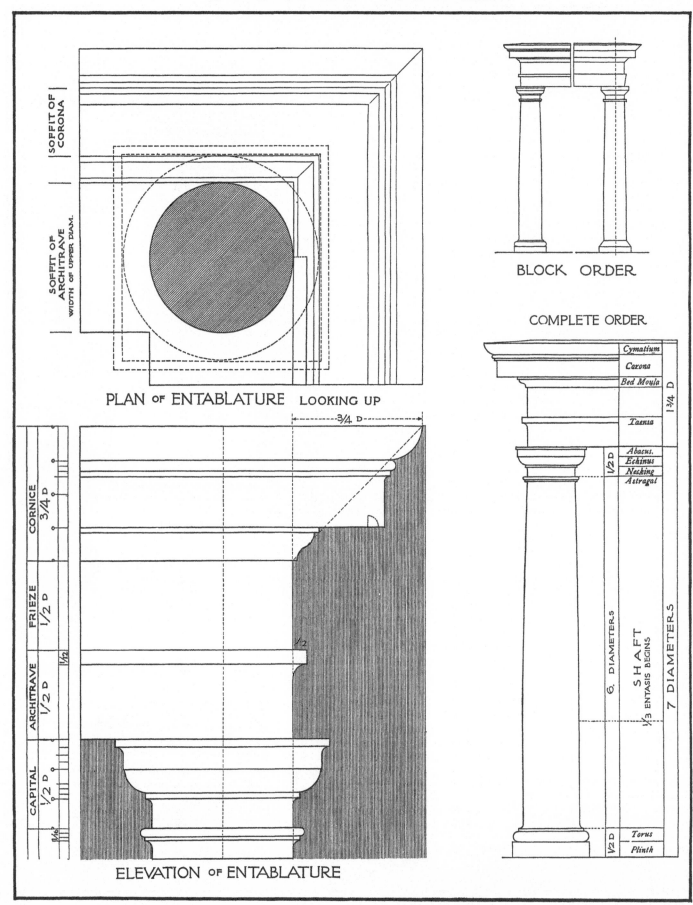

PLAN of ENTABLATURE LOOKING UP

BLOCK ORDER

COMPLETE ORDER

ELEVATION of ENTABLATURE

DORIC ORDER

PLATE V

PERSPECTIVE VIEW

DRAWN TO THE SCALE OF ORDER IN PLATE VI

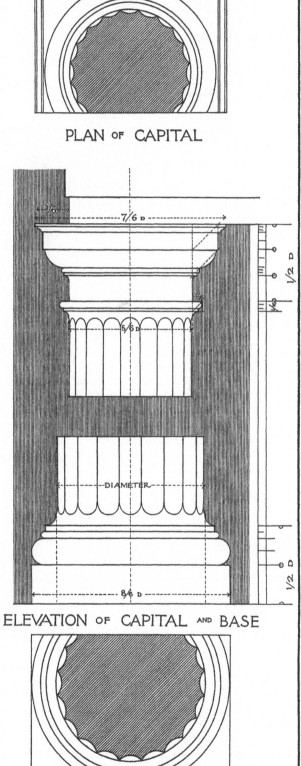

PLAN OF CAPITAL

7/6 D

1/2 D

5/6 D

DIAMETER

8/6 D

1/2 D

ELEVATION OF CAPITAL AND BASE

PLAN OF BASE

DORIC ORDER

PLATE VI

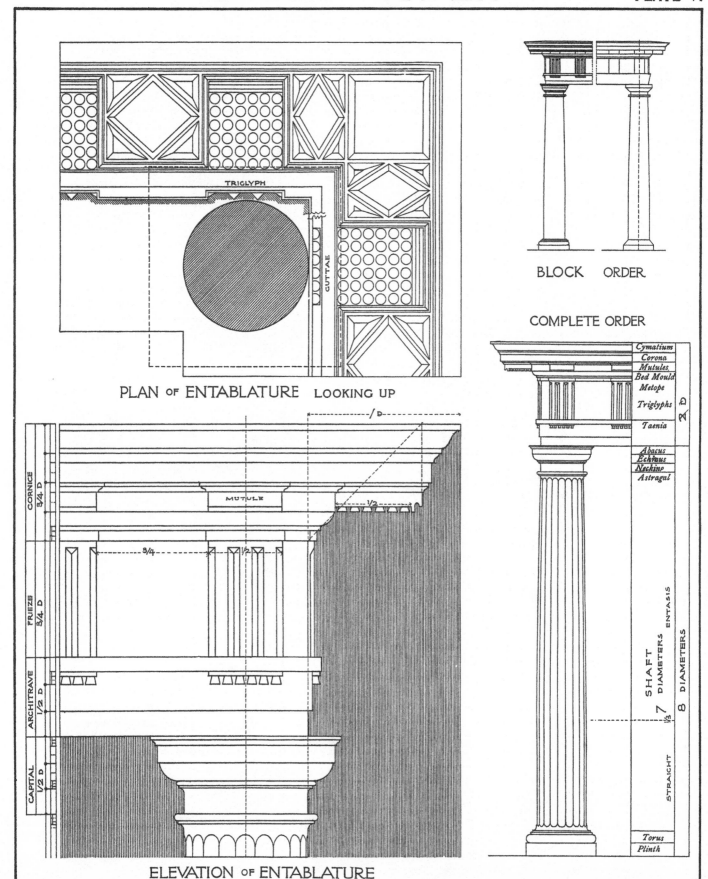

PLAN of ENTABLATURE LOOKING UP

BLOCK   ORDER

COMPLETE ORDER

ELEVATION of ENTABLATURE

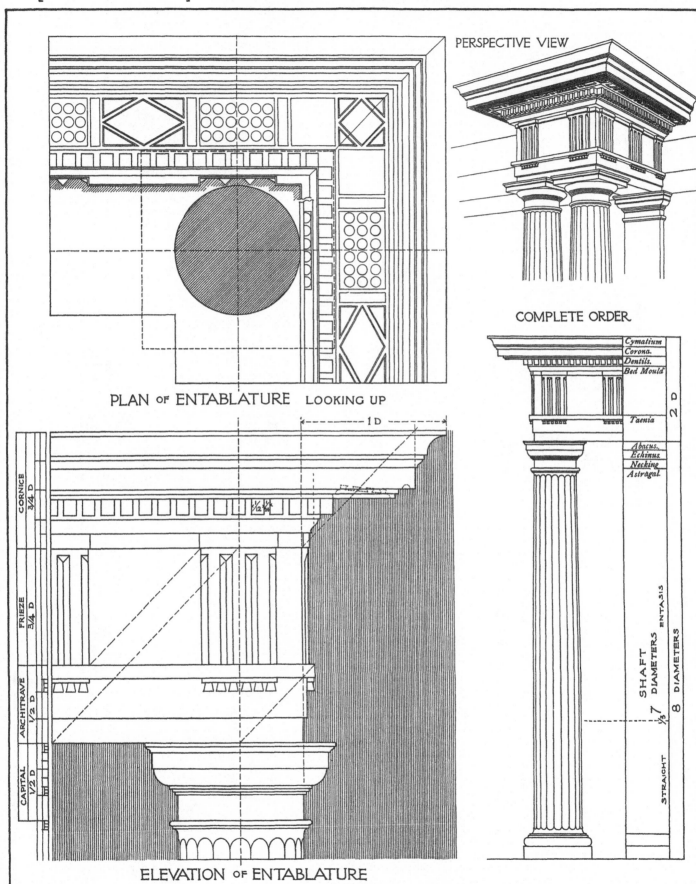

PERSPECTIVE VIEW

PLAN of ENTABLATURE LOOKING UP

COMPLETE ORDER

Cymatium
Corona.
Dentils.
Bed Mould

Taenia

2 D

Abacus.
Echinus.
Necking
Astragal.

CORNICE 3/4 D

FRIEZE 3/4 D

ARCHITRAVE 1/2 D

CAPITAL 1/2 D

1 D

SHAFT 7 DIAMETERS

ENTASIS

1/3

8 DIAMETERS

STRAIGHT

ELEVATION of ENTABLATURE

IONIC ORDER

PLATE VIII

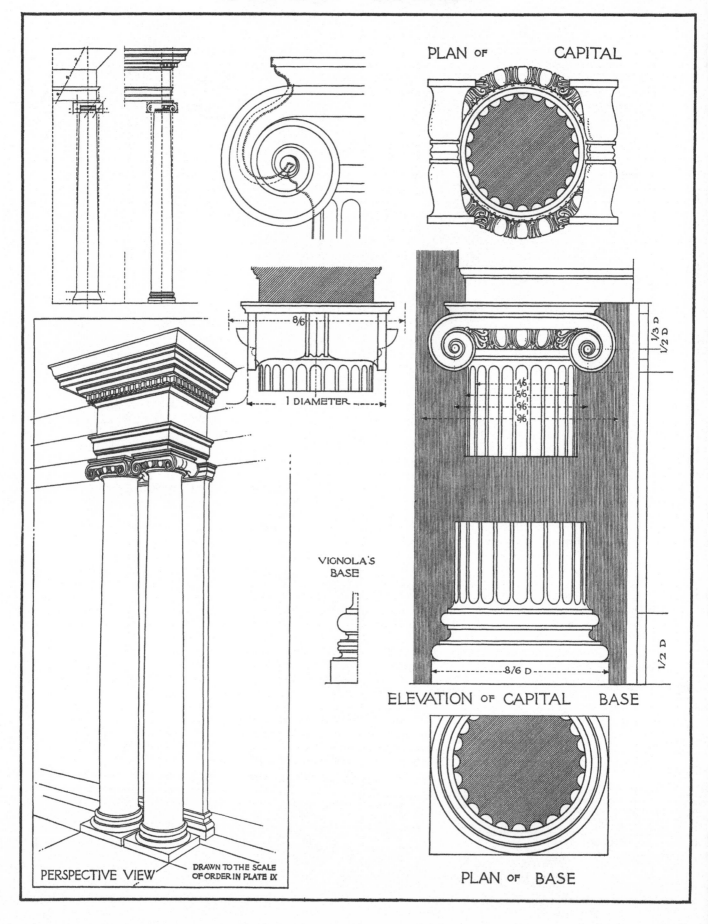

PLAN OF CAPITAL

8/6

1 DIAMETER

VIGNOLA'S BASE

4/6
5/6
6/6
9/6

1/3 D
1/2 D

8/6 D

1/2 D

ELEVATION OF CAPITAL BASE

PLAN OF BASE

PERSPECTIVE VIEW

DRAWN TO THE SCALE OF ORDER IN PLATE IX

IONIC ORDER

PLATE IX

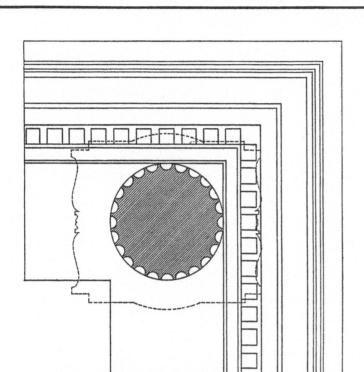

PLAN of ENTABLATURE LOOKING UP

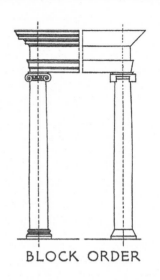

BLOCK ORDER

COMPLETE ORDER

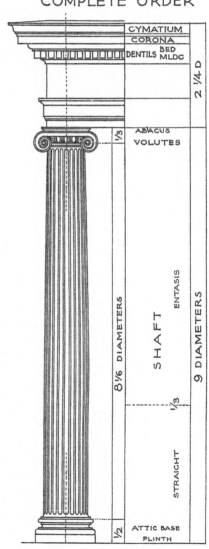

CYMATIUM
CORONA
DENTILS — BED MLDG
2 ¼ D

ABACUS
VOLUTES
1/3

8½ DIAMETERS

SHAFT — ENTASIS

9 DIAMETERS

STRAIGHT

1/3

ATTIC BASE
PLINTH
½

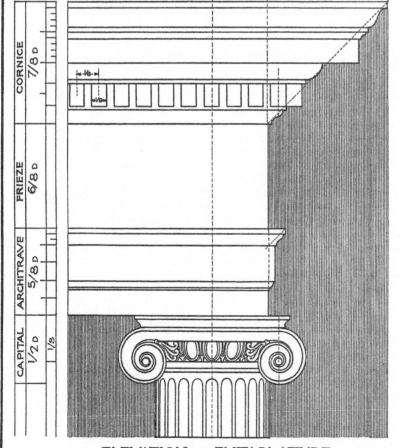

5/12 — 7/8

1/8

1/9

CORNICE 7/8 D

FRIEZE 6/8 D

ARCHITRAVE 5/8 D

CAPITAL ½ D — 1/3

ELEVATION of ENTABLATURE

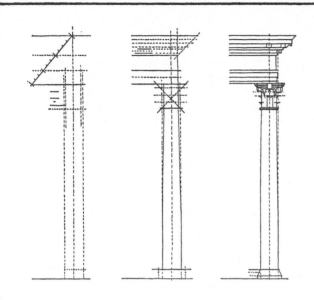

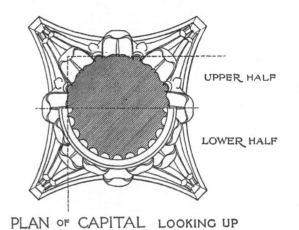

UPPER HALF

LOWER HALF

PLAN OF CAPITAL LOOKING UP

PERSPECTIVE VIEW

DRAWN TO THE SCALE OF ORDER IN PLATE XI

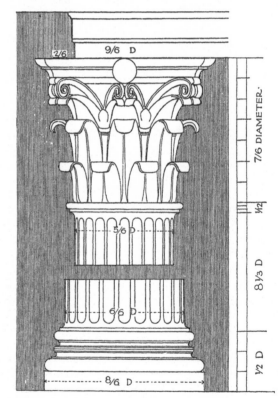

9/6 D

2/6

7/6 DIAMETER.

1/2

5/6 D

8 1/3 D

6/6 D

1/2 D

8/6 D

ELEVATION OF CAPITAL AND BASE

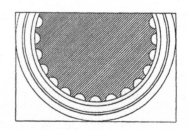

PLAN OF BASE

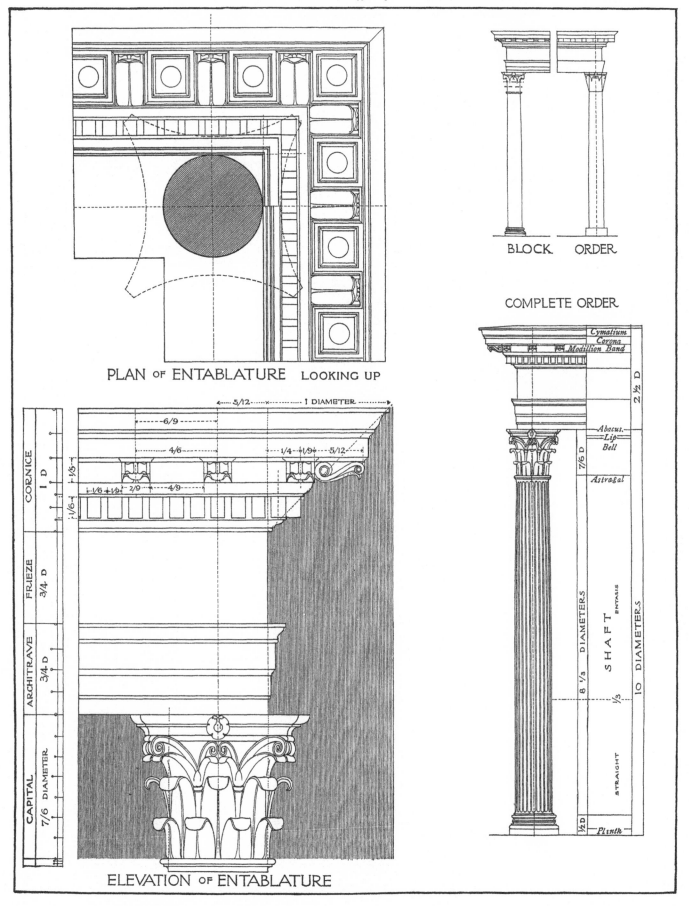

PLAN OF ENTABLATURE LOOKING UP

BLOCK ORDER

COMPLETE ORDER

ELEVATION OF ENTABLATURE

COMPOSITE ORDER

PLATE XII

AFTER VIGNOLA

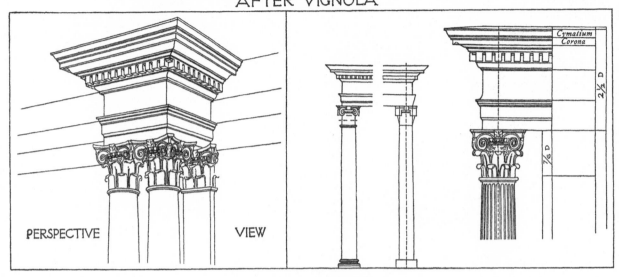

PERSPECTIVE VIEW

Cymatium
Corona

2½ D

⅙ D

AFTER PALLADIO

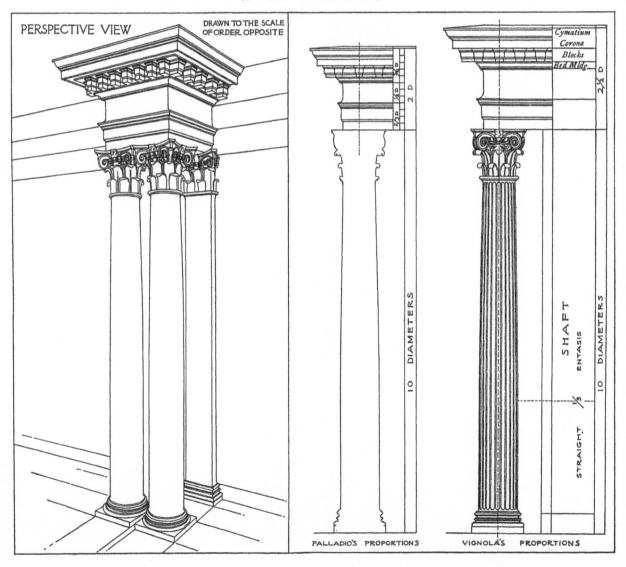

PERSPECTIVE VIEW

DRAWN TO THE SCALE
OF ORDER OPPOSITE

Cymatium
Corona
Blocks
Bed Mldg.

2½ D

2 D

⅔ D

10 DIAMETERS

SHAFT

ENTASIS

⅓

STRAIGHT

10 DIAMETERS

PALLADIO'S PROPORTIONS

VIGNOLA'S PROPORTIONS

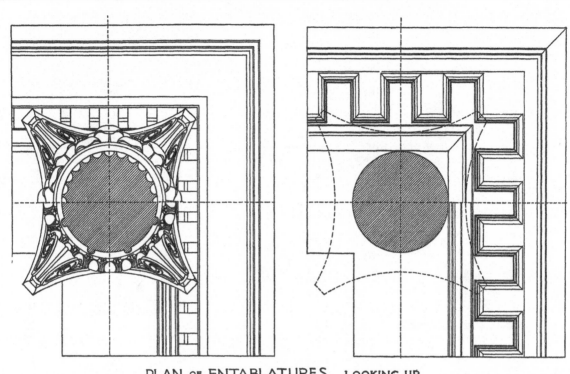

PLAN OF ENTABLATURES LOOKING UP

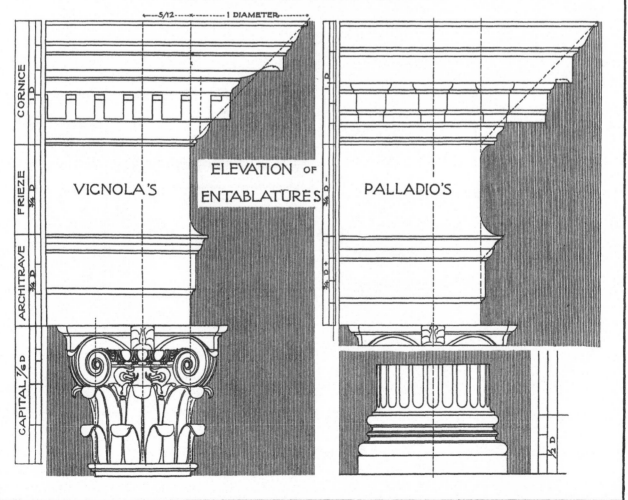

←—5/12—→←————— 1 DIAMETER —————→

CORNICE 1 D

FRIEZE ¾ D

ARCHITRAVE ¾ D

CAPITAL ⅞ D

VICNOLA'S

ELEVATION OF ENTABLATURES

PALLADIO'S

1 D

¾ D

¾ D+

½ D

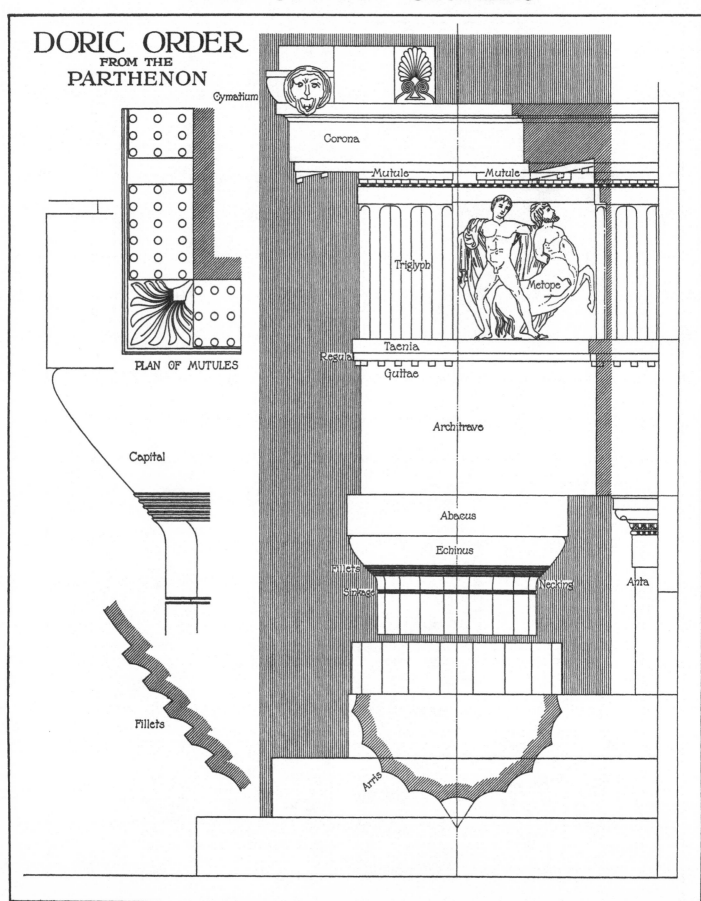

DORIC ORDER
FROM THE
PARTHENON

Cymatium

PLAN OF MUTULES

Capital

Fillets

Corona

Mutule   Mutule

Triglyph

Metope

Taenia

Regula

Guttae

Architrave

Abacus

Echinus

Fillets

Sinkage   Neckins   Anta

Arris

IONIC ORDER
FROM THE TEMPLE
ON THE ILLISSUS

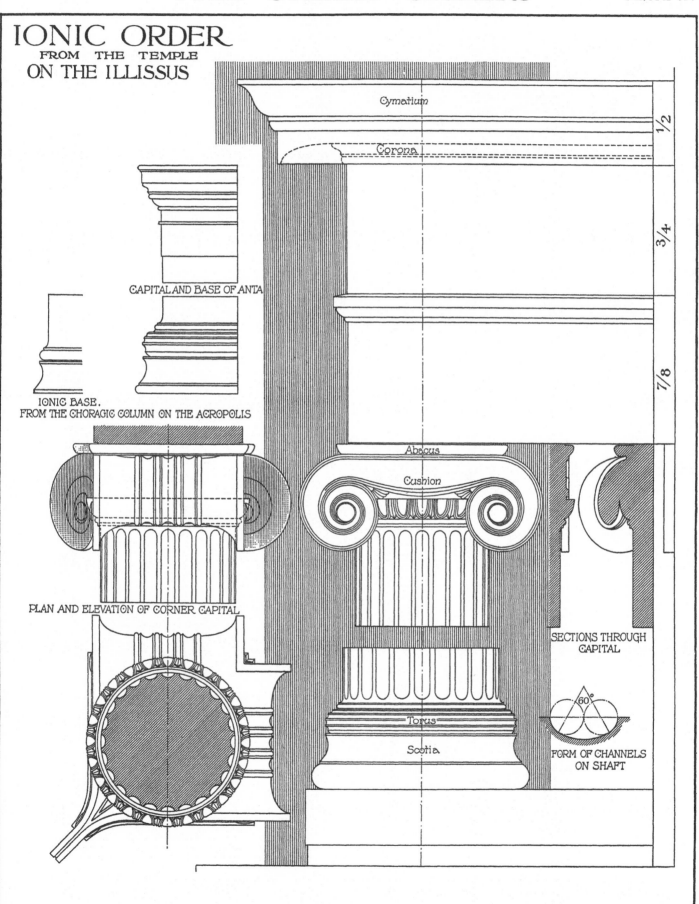

CAPITAL AND BASE OF ANTA

IONIC BASE.
FROM THE CHORAGIC COLUMN ON THE ACROPOLIS

Cymatium

Corona

1/2

3/4

7/8

Abacus

Cushion

PLAN AND ELEVATION OF CORNER CAPITAL

SECTIONS THROUGH
CAPITAL

Torus

Scotia

60°

FORM OF CHANNELS
ON SHAFT

PLATE XVI

PEDESTALS AND PILASTERS

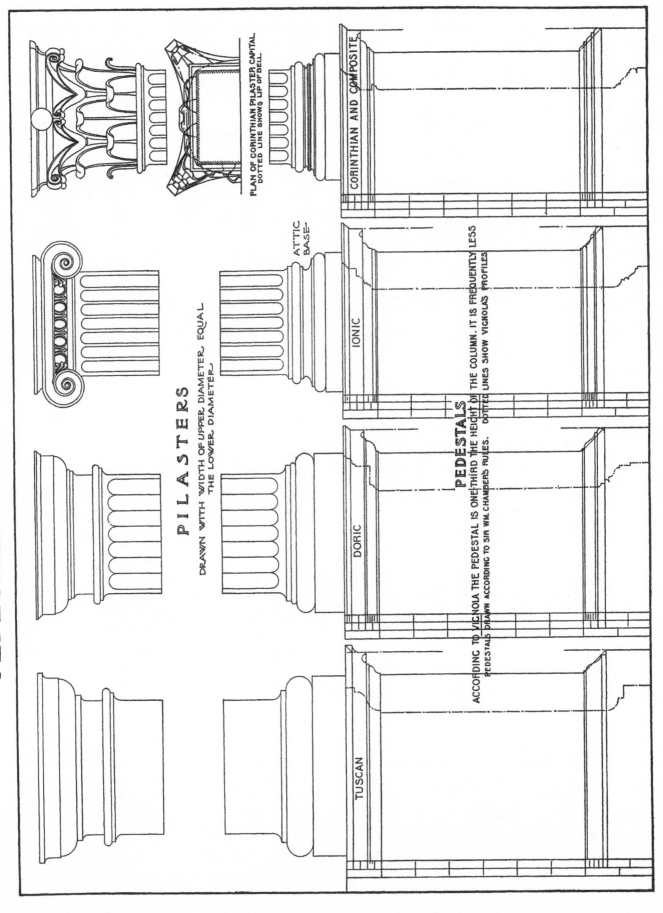

PILASTERS

DRAWN WITH WIDTH OF UPPER DIAMETER EQUAL THE LOWER DIAMETER

PLAN OF CORINTHIAN PILASTER CAPITAL
DOTTED LINE SHOWS LIP OF BELL

ATTIC BASE

CORINTHIAN AND COMPOSITE

IONIC

DORIC

TUSCAN

PEDESTALS

ACCORDING TO VIGNOLA THE PEDESTAL IS ONE-THIRD THE HEIGHT OF THE COLUMN. IT IS FREQUENTLY LESS
PEDESTALS DRAWN ACCORDING TO SIR WM. CHAMBER'S RULES.   DOTTED LINES SHOW VIGNOLA'S PROFILES

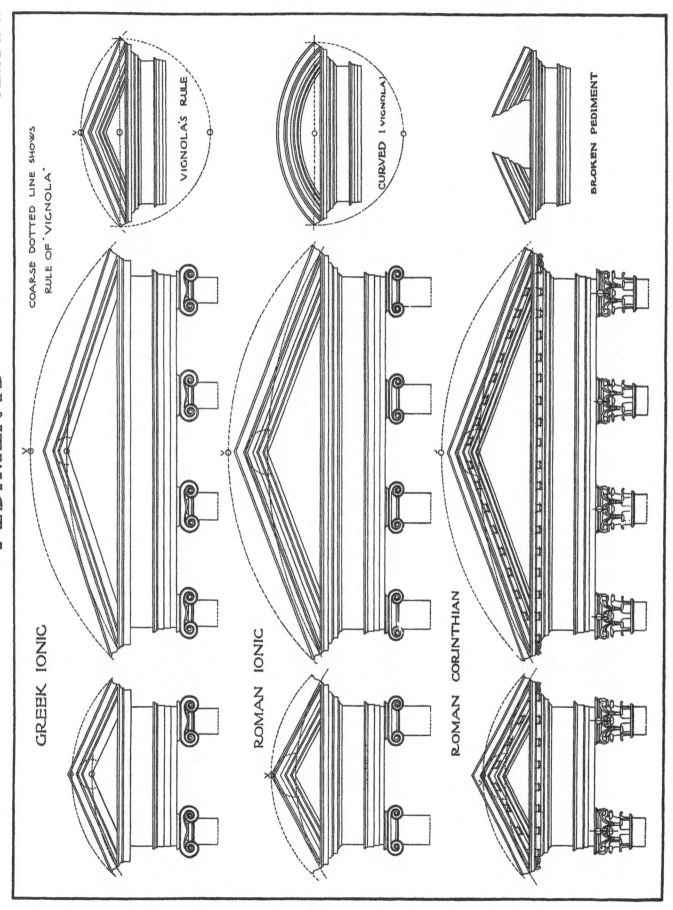

PLATE XVII

PEDIMENTS

VIGNOLA'S RULE

CURVED (VIGNOLA)

BROKEN PEDIMENT

COARSE DOTTED LINE SHOWS RULE OF "VIGNOLA"

GREEK IONIC

ROMAN IONIC

ROMAN CORINTHIAN

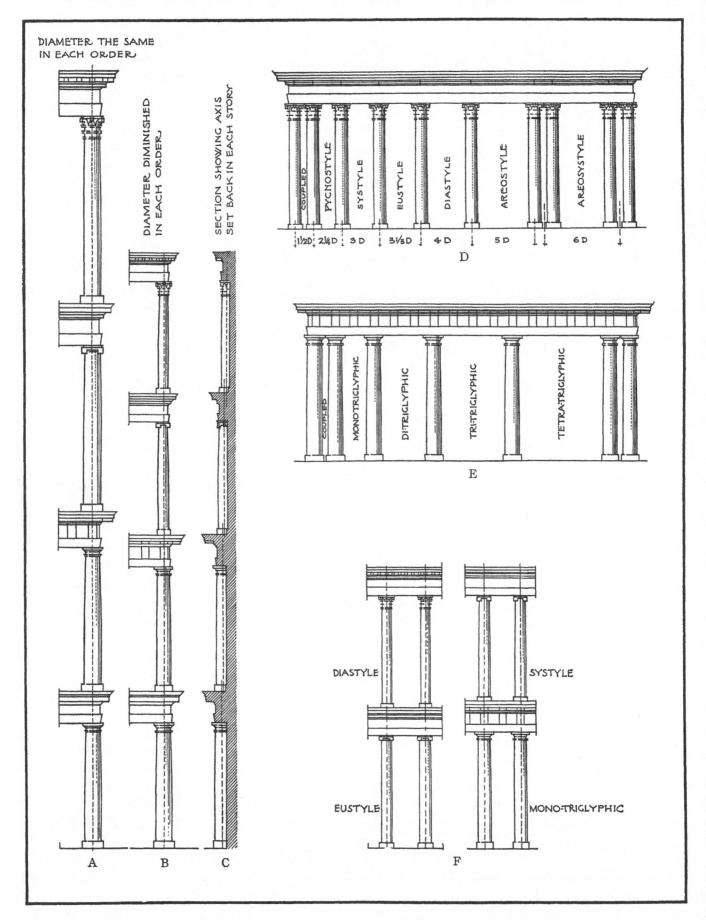

DIAMETER THE SAME IN EACH ORDER

DIAMETER DIMINISHED IN EACH ORDER

SECTION SHOWING AXIS SET BACK IN EACH STORY

A   B   C

COUPLED PYCNOSTYLE SYSTYLE EUSTYLE DIASTYLE AREOSTYLE AREOSYSTYLE

1½D 2¼D 3 D 3⅓D 4 D 5 D 6 D

D

COUPLED MONOTRIGLYPHIC DI-TRIGLYPHIC TRI-TRIGLYPHIC TETRA-TRIGLYPHIC

E

DIASTYLE   SYSTYLE

EUSTYLE   MONO-TRIGLYPHIC

F

PART II

Arches and Vaults
Roofs and Domes
Doors and Windows
Walls and Ceilings
Steps and Staircases

PREFACE

THE First Part of this work, which was published three years ago, treated of the Five Roman Orders, and presented a simple method of drawing them, in accordance with the proportions determined by Vignola. Chapters were added on the Intercolumniation and Superposition of Columns, and on Parapets, Balustrades, String-Courses, Pediments, and Attics.

In the Preface I said that the employment of these Elements in the composition of Doors and Windows, Wall Surfaces, Staircases, Towers and Spires, Arches and Arcades, Vaults and Domes, might some day be made the subject of a separate treatise which would be the natural sequel of the first. The present publication fulfils this promise, except that Towers and Spires are not among the topics taken up. It contains also, under the heading of Wall Treatment, a discussion of Coupled Pilasters, and of the treatment of Pilasters and of Cornices on external and internal angles, which might perhaps just as well have been put into the other volume.

Of the Nineteen Plates placed at the end of the book, three are taken from Sir William Chambers' *Civil Architecture*, though the figuring of the orders is simplified, in accordance with the system set forth in Part I. One Plate is taken from Gruner's *Fresco Painting in Italy*, one from the Comte de Clarac's *Louvre and Tuileries*, and one from Letarouilly's *Edifices de Rome Moderne*. Of the hundred and three illustrations inserted in the Text, half a dozen, and an equal number of the figures in some of the Plates, have been copied or traced from various works of reference. The remainder of the Plates and Figures have been drawn out from sketches or made under my direction. For the sympathetic care and skill with which this work has been done I am much indebted to the young men who have divided the work among them, and am under special obligations to Mr. G. L. Smith, Mr. H. V. Skene, Mr. F. M. Riley, and Mr. Joseph Wilson, for serviceable criticisms and suggestions.

Milton, Massachusetts, October 1, 1905

WILLIAM R. WARE

THE AMERICAN VIGNOLA
PART II

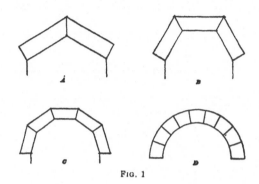

T HE First Part of this work treated of the Five Orders of classical Roman Architecture, of the Greek Orders, and of Pilasters, Pediments, Pedestals, and Attics, of the Intercolumniation and Superposition of Columns, and of Moldings and String-Courses. The present volume treats of Arches and Arcades, Vaults and Domes, Doors and Windows, Walls and Ceilings, and of Staircases, including the use of the Orders in these various features.

FIG. 1

ARCHES

As was said in Part I, an opening in a wall may be spanned by a single beam of wood, stone, or iron, bearing vertically on the points of support. It carries the weight of the beam itself and of whatever rests upon it. This beam is called an *Architrave*, or, sometimes, if it rests upon columns, an *Epistyle*. If the opening is spanned by two or more such beams, leaning against and mutually supporting each other, the structure is called an *Arch* (Fig. 1, *A, B, C,* and *D*). An arch not only throws its own weight and that of the load it carries upon the piers or columns that support it, but it also exerts upon them a horizontal thrust, which tends to push them apart and overthrow them. This thrust has to be met either by a horizontal tie of wood, stone, or iron, at the level of the spring of the arch, or by a sufficiently strong pier, or wall, to serve as an abutment, or buttress (Figs. 2 and 3).

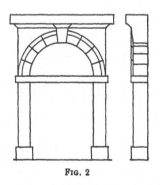

FIG. 2

The separate stones of which an arch is composed are called its *Voussoirs*. The joints that separate them are at right angles to the inner curve of the arch, which is called the *Intrados*. The outer curve, or back of the arch, is called its *Extrados* (Fig. 3 *A*).

The joints between the voussoirs and the curved joint at the extrados are not generally recognized as architectural features, any more than are the joints between the other stones of which a wall is built up. When they are so recognized, and the shape of the stones or of the voussoirs is made conspicuous, the masonry is said to be *Rusticated* (Fig. 50). Rustication and Rusticated Arches are treated on page 18.

But the line of the extrados, like other lines that it may be considered desirable to emphasize, is generally marked by a raised molding, similar to the Tænia or Cymatium that

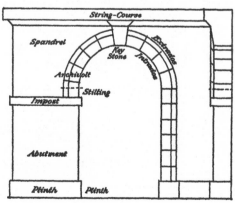

FIG. 3 (*A*)

75

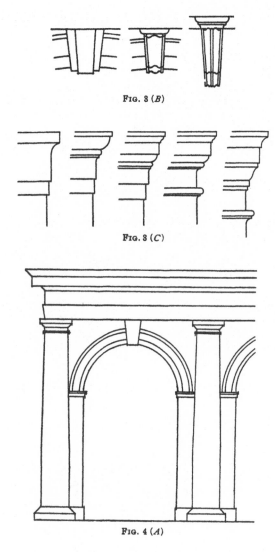

FIG. 3 (B)

FIG. 3 (C)

FIG. 4 (A)

FIG. 4 (B)

marks the upper line of the Architrave. The face of the arch and the molding that thus circumscribes it are called the *Archivolt*. It is often composed, in imitation of the Architrave, of several bands, or fascias, with or without small moldings, or cymatia, between them (Figs. 3 and 4).

When the face of the wall that an arch supports is marked, just above the arch, by a horizontal member, or *String-Course* (Fig. 3 *A*), the upper voussoir of the arch is generally extended so as to reach and apparently support it, and it is often made to project beyond the others both in front and below, and is frequently fashioned into the shape of a corbel, console, bracket, or modillion. When thus emphasized, it is called a *Keystone*. Keystones should be higher than they are wide. They are sometimes triple. Fig. 3 *B* shows those adopted by Vignola for Doric and Corinthian arches. He omits keystones in the Tuscan and Doric arches, but in this his example has not been generally followed.

Such a string-course is sometimes, especially at the top of a wall, treated like an architrave and surmounted by a Frieze and Cornice (Fig. 4). The horizontal joint at the top of the pier, at the spring of the arch, is also generally marked by a molding, which is called an *Impost;* and at the foot of the pier is a plinth, with or without base moldings. The pier thus treated closely resembles a Tuscan or Doric pilaster, with its capital and base, or a tall pedestal; and, as in pedestal caps, a cyma recta is often used in the bed mold instead of an ovolo. Fig. 3 *C* shows forms of imposts adopted by Vignola and Palladio. In very large arches a full entablature is sometimes used without a frieze. The top of the Impost comes naturally at the level of the center of the arch, but it is often set a little lower, so that the full semicircle may be seen above it. In this case, the arch is said to be *Stilted* (Fig. 3 *A*).

The fragment of triangular or trapezoidal wall at the side of the arch and above the Impost is called the *Spandrel*.

When the Impost is omitted, the moldings of the archivolt are continued down the pier (Fig. 3 *A*).

When a full entablature occurs just above an arch, resting upon its keystone, the face of the pier is often decorated with a pilaster, with or without a pedestal, which runs up as high as the top of the keystone and, like it, seems to support the architrave. In this case, the entablature and the pilaster may have the form and proportions of some one of the five regular Roman Orders. This combination of a full order with a wall pierced by an arch is called the Roman Arch, and sometimes the Roman Order (Fig. 4 *A* and *B*). The Greek Orders are not used with arches.

An arch may be made wider, without changing its height, by lowering the Impost, as in Fig. 5 *A*, and may be made higher, without changing its width, by lengthening the piers, as in Fig. 5 *B*. There is, in general, nothing to determine the shape of an archway, that is to say, to fix the proportion

between the width of an opening and its height, or the shape
of the piers that support it, except considerations of good
looks, strength, and convenience. But such a change of proportions naturally takes place in the Roman Orders merely by
the change in the length of the pilasters, from seven diameters in the Tuscan to ten in the Corinthian and Composite.
The piers, reckoning their height up to the architraves, then
vary in shape from about two diameters by eight to two
diameters by thirteen, that is, from four times their height
to about seven times. If the width of the arches were kept
the same, the shape of the opening would change in like
manner, from the proportion of about four diameters by
eight to four diameters by thirteen, or from two squares
to three or four. But it is customary, in the more slender
arches, to diminish this attenuation by widening the opening, thus lengthening the radius of the arch and lowering
the impost.

In antiquity, the openings in the Triumphal Arches vary
in the ratio of width to height from about six to seven, or
nearly square, in the arch at Rimini, to nearly one to three,
in the arch at Ancona, the shape of the opening in each
case following the general shape of the entire structure.

Elliptical Arches.—When elliptical arches are employed in
place of semicircular ones, harmony of shape requires that
the archways and piers, as well as the arch itself, shall
be comparatively broad and low. The greater thrust of an
elliptical arch also requires a wider pier (Fig. 6 *A*).

Segmental Arches.—The same considerations apply to
Segmental Arches. Segmental Arches need to be stilted, to
prevent an awkward meeting of the archivolt and the
impost (Fig. 6 *B*).

Palladio's Motive.—In the arcades with which he surrounded the old Basilica at Vincenza, Andrea Palladio introduced a scheme that has since been known by his name (Fig. 7).
The archivolt is supported by a small column that carries,
for an impost, an entablature of two members, that is, an
architrave and cornice, without any frieze. The other end
of this architrave rests upon a pilaster, set some distance
away and set edgewise, facing the small columns. This is
backed by a large pilaster that runs as high as the top of the
keystone of the arch and helps carry a large entablature.
The space on each side, bounded by the arch and the pilaster
and by the small entablature below and the large one above,
is filled by a trapezoidal spandrel.

Roman Arches Without Pedestals.—*Plate I.*—But in the
Roman Arch, in which the piers are decorated with a pilaster
or column, it is customary to make the archway about twice
as high as it is wide, or "two squares," and the pier about half
this width, or, in the Tuscan Order, a little more. If there
is no pedestal, the pilaster is made half as wide as the pier,
and its height is made the same as that of the archway. The
face of the pier on each side of the pilaster is thus half a

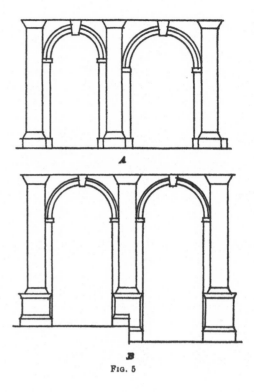

FIG. 5

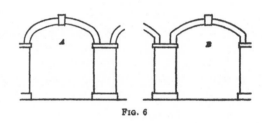

FIG. 6

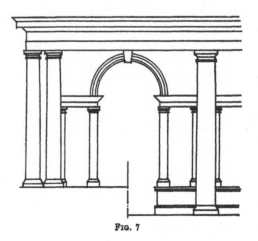

FIG. 7

diameter wide. Beneath the pilaster is set a block, or extra plinth, three-quarters of a diameter high (or a whole diameter), and there is accordingly an equal space of three-quarters of a diameter (or an entire diameter) between the top of the opening and the entablature above it. The archivolt is half a diameter wide. There is thus a space of either a quarter of a diameter or half a diameter between the extrados of the arch and the architrave above it, and the keystone is made longer than the other voussoirs by this amount.

It follows that the pier, up to the top of the impost, is about one-third as wide as the opening, which makes it about three squares high. The rectangular part of the opening, between the piers, is two-thirds as wide as it is high. These proportions obtain with exactness for the Ionic Order. In the Tuscan and Doric the opening of the archway is made a little wider, and in the Corinthian and Composite it is a little narrower, so as to be in harmony with their general character of greater heaviness or lightness (Plate I).

But here, as in the spacing of columns, and indeed as in the proportions of the Orders themselves, usage greatly varies, and authorities differ.

The proportions of the Doric Arch, however, are closely determined by the necessity of having a triglyph over each pilaster. Since the triglyphs are spaced one and one-fourth diameters on centers, the distance from axis to axis of the piers must be a multiple of one and one-fourth diameters. The best dimension is six and one-fourth diameters. This gives four triglyphs over the arch, besides the two over the pilasters, or six in all. The arches are four and one-fourth diameters in breadth by eight diameters high, or a little less than two squares. The Tuscan Arch (Plate I, *A*), which is seven diameters high, is made still wider in proportion, measuring three and three-fourths diameters.

As it is desirable to have a dentil come over each pilaster, and it is necessary that a modillion should, the distance of the Ionic pilasters on centers, must be a multiple of one-sixth of a diameter, and of the Corinthian, a multiple of two-thirds of a diameter. The opening of the Ionic Arch (Plate I, *C*) is generally made four and one-half diameters, or just half its height. This sets the pilasters six and one-half diameters on centers, or thirty-nine sixths of a diameter, which gives thirty-eight dentils over the arch, besides the two over the pilasters and three more outside at each end, making forty-six in all.

The Corinthian Arch (Plate I, *D*) is made a little more than two squares high, the height being ten diameters and the width only four and two-thirds diameters, the pilasters being six and two-thirds diameters on centers, or forty sixths of a diameter. This gives one more dentil than for the Ionic Arch and nine modillions over the arch, besides the two over the pilasters and one more at each end, or thirteen in all.

If Vignola's Composite is used, with dentils one-fourth of a diameter on centers, the opening had better be four and one-half diameters in width (or four and three-fourths), giving room for twenty-five (or twenty-six) dentils over the arch besides six others, making thirty-one (or thirty-two) in all. In Palladio's Composite Order, in which the distance apart of the blocks on centers varies considerably in different examples, the distance apart of the axes of the pilasters should be some multiple of that distance.

The proportions of the four arches shown in Plate I are those adopted by Sir William Chambers. They follow closely those published by Vignola, and conform to the figures just given. In all four, the height of the opening is just the height of the pilaster. The pilaster stands upon a plinth three-fourths of a diameter in height, and the width of the pier is two diameters, showing a half diameter on each side of the pilaster, just enough to receive the archivolt, which is, in every case, a half diameter in width.

*Roman Arches With Pedestals.—Plate II.—*When the pilaster stands upon a pedestal, instead of upon an extra plinth, the size and shape of the archway and of the piers are substantially unchanged. But since the pedestal takes up about a quarter of the height, being regularly one-third the height of the column, the scale of the whole order is one-fourth smaller. The diameter of the shaft, and the height of the pilaster and of the entablature, are only about three-fourths as great as when there is no pedestal. The pilaster being thus narrowed, the plain face of the pier, left on each side of it, is somewhat wider, measuring five-eighths of the new diameter instead of one-half of the old one. In the Tuscan order (Plate II, *A*), the pier is more than half the width of the opening, but in the others it is less. For though, relatively to the pilaster, the pier is one-third longer, it is only one-eighth wider. The piers with pedestals are thus of more slender proportions than those without pedestals.

Here, again, the proportions of the Doric Arch (Plate II, *B*) are predetermined, since the distance of the pilasters, on centers, must be a multiple of one and one-fourth diameters, so as to bring a triglyph over each pilaster. The only convenient arrangement is to have five triglyphs over the arch, which, with two over the pilasters, makes seven in all. This brings a triglyph in the middle, over the keystone. The distance apart of the pilasters, on centers, is just seven and one-half diameters, and if, as usual, the pier is two and one-fourth diameters in width, the opening of the arch is five and one-fourth diameters wide by ten and two-thirds diameters high, or a little more than two squares. But Sir William Chambers, as appears in the Plate, makes the pedestal two and one-fourth diameters high instead of two and two-thirds, diminishing the height by three-twelfths of a diameter. This makes the height of the opening exactly nine and one-half diameters.

In like manner, he reduces the Tuscan pedestal from two and one-third diameters to two diameters; the Ionic, from three diameters to two and one-half diameters; and the Corinthian, from three and one-third diameters to three diameters.

Here, again, the width of the opening must be such that the Ionic and Corinthian pilasters shall come exactly under a dentil or modillion; that is, the distance of the Ionic pilasters, on centers, must be a multiple of one-sixth of a diameter, and that of the Corinthian pilasters a multiple of four-sixths of a diameter. The Ionic pilasters (Plate II, *C*) are accordingly set eight diameters on centers, or forty-eight sixths of a diameter. This gives forty-seven dentils over the arch, which, with the one over each pilaster and three at each end, makes fifty-five in all. The Corinthian pilasters (Plate II, *D*) are set eight and two-thirds diameters on centers, or fifty-two sixths of a diameter, which gives four more dentils than to the Ionic, and twelve modillions over the arch, making sixteen modillions altogether.

When there is no pedestal, the height of the opening is fixed, being the same as the height of the pilaster, and the only way of changing the shape of the opening is to change the width—either increasing it by lowering the impost and so lengthening the radius of the arch, or diminishing it by raising the impost and adopting a smaller radius—as has been said, and as is illustrated in Fig. 5 *A*. But when there is a pedestal, the shape of the opening may be changed without altering the width, by simply changing the height of the pedestal, as in the plate. This is exemplified in the Arch at Ancona, and by the lofty entrance erected by Lombardi in front of the church of Sta. Francesca Romana, near the Roman Forum.

*Superposition of Arches.—Plate III.—*When Roman arches are superposed, they follow the same rule that governs the superposition of colonnades. The lower diameter of the upper column or pilaster is equal to the upper diameter of the lower one. If the Diminution is, as usual, one-sixth of a diameter, it follows that the scale of the upper order is five-sixths that of the lower one. As the upper pilasters are set exactly over the lower ones, their distance on centers, as expressed in terms of the upper diameter, is six-fifths of the same distance expressed in terms of the lower diameter.

Plate III shows three examples of superposed Roman arches and one example of superposed Palladian Motives, according to Sir William Chambers. In each case, the upper order has a pedestal. Each order is figured in terms of the diameter of its own column. As in Plate II, the height of the pedestals is less than one-third the height of the columns they carry.

Here, as in the case of single arches, the pilasters must be set at such a distance on centers as shall bring a triglyph or a modillion exactly upon the axis of the pier. The best arrangement is to set the pilasters of the lower order six and one-fourth diameters on centers, and those of the upper order seven and one-half diameters. Six and one-fourth is five-sixths of seven and one-half, so that seven and one-half times the smaller diameter equals six and one-fourth times the larger one.

This works perfectly well where the Doric order is superposed upon the Tuscan (Plate III, *A*), and the Ionic upon the Doric (Plate III, *B*). But where the Corinthian arch is placed over the Ionic (Plate III, *C*), the Corinthian pilasters must be eight diameters on centers instead of seven and one-half diameters, since eight is a multiple of two-thirds, the distance on centers of the modillion, while seven and one-half is not. The Ionic pilasters below are then six and two-thirds diameters on centers, instead of six and one-fourth, six and two-thirds being five-sixths of eight. This gives room for thirty-nine dentils over the Ionic arch which is beneath the Corinthian one, or forty-seven in all; and room also for forty-four, or fifty-two altogether, over the Ionic arch which is above the Doric one. The Corinthian arch has fifteen modillions, instead of sixteen as in Plate II.

The lower arches are all less than two squares high, the Tuscan and Ionic openings being a little wider than when arches without pedestals are used alone. If the pedestals of the upper orders are made one-third as high as the pilasters they support, the upper arches are all more than two squares high. But these pedestals are commonly, as in the Plate, only one-fourth or one-fifth the height of the column. This makes

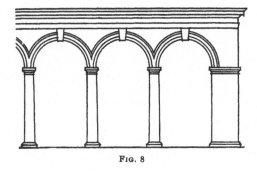

FIG. 8

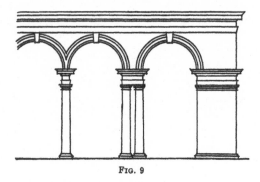

FIG. 9

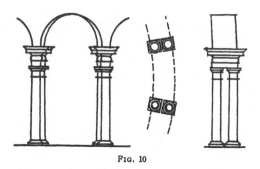

FIG. 10

the Corinthian arch exactly two squares high, and the Ionic one very nearly so.

If a Corinthian arch is set above a Doric arch, which seldom happens, either the modillions must be set nearer together or the triglyphs set farther apart, or both.

When an Ionic Palladian Motive is set over a Doric one, as in Plate III, *D*, there are seven triglyphs in the Doric entablature, and the Doric pilasters are set seven and a half diameters on centers, just as in the arch with pedestals. The Ionic pilasters are nine diameters on centers, nine being six-fifths of seven and a half, and there is room, altogether, for sixty dentils.

Arcades.—A series of arches resting upon piers is called an *Arcade*. The arches sometimes come down upon a single column, instead of upon piers (Fig. 8). One of the earliest examples of this treatment is an arcade in the Palace of Diocletian at Spalato in Dalmatia, built about the year 325 A. D. But in medieval and modern times it is common. The intrados comes in line with the upper diameter of the column, and if the width of the archivolt is more than five-twelfths of the lower diameter, the two cymatia intersect one another (Fig. 9).

Sometimes the place of the pier is taken by coupled columns, which in this case generally carry a fragment of architrave, or even of a full entablature, which serves as a sort of impost to receive the archivolts, very much as in Palladio's Motive (Fig. 9). This is often used with single columns.

Sometimes, as in the Baptistry of Sta. Constanza, in Rome, and at St. Sulpice, in Paris, the coupled columns are set across the wall (Fig. 10).

But a column, or even two columns, is an insufficient abutment, and an arcade must end in a pier, if it terminates at an external angle or corner, as in Figs. 8 and 9.

At the internal angle of a courtyard or cloister, also, something firmer than a single column is needed, such as a pier, either square or L-shaped, or at least a group of three columns (Fig. 72).

VAULTS

An arch spans an opening in a wall, serving the purpose of a beam, and is no thicker than the wall itself. It carries not only its own weight, but the weight of the portion of wall above it, and has the adjacent portions of the wall as natural abutments. A *Vault* is a sort of deep arch. But it differs from an arch in that it is not used to effect passage through a wall, but answers the purpose of a floor to cover a space. It has little more than its own weight to carry, but it has no natural abutments, and tends to push over the walls that support it.

The simplest form of vault is the *Barrel*, or *Cylindrical, vault*, as shown in *A*, Fig. 11. This, like the arch, may be semicircular, elliptical, or segmental. Either kind may be reenforced or strengthened by transverse arches, of somewhat smaller radius, erected from point to point within them, which, being better buttressed, add firmness to the construction (Fig. 11 *B* and Fig. 12).

Barrel Vaults, and the Groined and Cloistered Vaults which are composed of them, are commonly built up in horizontal courses, the horizontal joints being the continuous ones (Fig. 13). But in Egyptian and Assyrian vaulting, and in the Byzantine vaulting which is derived from it, the vertical joints are the continuous ones, so that the vault consists of a succession of narrow arches, set side by side (Figs. 14 and 15).

Intersecting Cylinders.—*Plate IV.*—When equal horizontal semicylinders intersect, the square they cover in common is twice covered, the lines of intersection being two vertical semiellipses crossing the square from corner to corner, and cutting each vault into four triangular segments (Plate IV, *A*). If, now, we suppose the two lower portions of each to be removed, we have left the two upper segments of each, and the four have the form of what is called a *Groined Arch*, or *Vault* (Plate IV, *B*). If we suppose the four upper triangles to be removed, the four lower ones constitute what is called a *Cloistered*, or *Closed*, *Arch*, or *Vault* (Plate IV, *C*). The Groined Vault is open on all sides, and rests upon four piers at the corners. The Cloistered Arch is closed on all sides, and rests upon the four walls that enclose it. A section through the Groined Arch shows the vaulted surface lying between the horizontal line of the ridge above and the curved line of the vault below. A section through the Cloistered Arch shows the vaulted surface bounded by the curved line of the vault above and the horizontal line of the springing below.

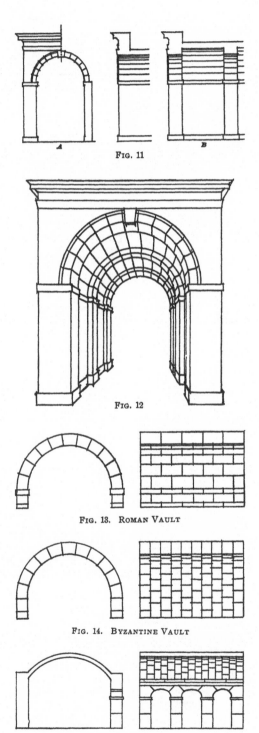

FIG. 11

FIG. 12

FIG. 13. ROMAN VAULT

FIG. 14. BYZANTINE VAULT

FIG. 15. CISTERN IN JERUSALEM

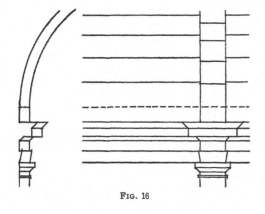

FIG. 16

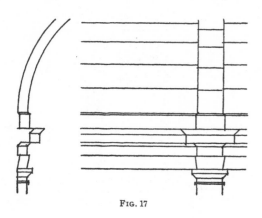

FIG. 17

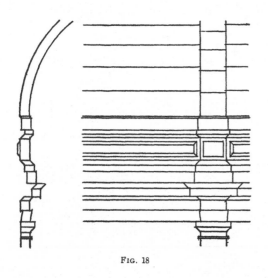

FIG. 18

The solid angle upon the elliptical line at the intersection of cylindrical vaults measures 90 degrees at the spring of the ellipse, but grows flatter as it rises. This angle is salient in the Groined Arch, and is called the *Groin*. In the Cloistered Arch it retreats, forming a reentering angle, and may be called a *Hollow Groin*.

Groined Arches, and Corridors.—Plates V and VI.—A corridor, or passage, can conveniently be covered either by a barrel vault, or by a series of groined vaults, formed by the intersection of a longitudinal barrel vault and transverse barrel vaults of the same size (Plate V, *A*). It is better not to have the groined vaults absolutely touch one another, but to have a short segment of barrel vault intervene. This space may, if desired, be occupied by a transverse arch, concentric with the longitudinal barrel vault, but of somewhat smaller radius, and supported by a pilaster at each end, as at *B*. A similar arch may be formed in the wall of the corridor, concentric with the transverse barrel arch, and also supported by pilasters, as at *C*, making on each side of the corridor a group of three pilasters.

It is to be noted in all these cases that the elliptical groin, on the line of the diagonal, springs from the hollow corner between the pilasters, that each bay of the vault is an exact square, and that the width of the corridor is the same as that of the intersecting vaults.

Plate VI shows the slightly different treatment of the same problem that presents itself when the width of the corridor is slightly greater than that of the intersecting barrel vaults. Here, as before, the successive transverse arches and the groined vaults do not quite touch. A short piece of barrel vault separates them. But as the corridor is a little wider than the longitudinal vault, the transverse vault terminates on each side in a short section of barrel vault. These sections all rest upon short sections of wall that are virtually piers, as at *A*. If the groined vaults are set a little farther apart, as at *B*, a transverse arch of smaller radius can, as before, be thrown across the passage, making groups of three pilasters, and still others, as at *C*, can be placed along the walls, making groups of five pilasters.

It is to be noted that in these cases the elliptical diagonal groin springs from the projecting corner of the pilaster, and that each bay of the vault is of the shape of a Greek cross. Also, that while in the first case, as shown in Plate V, we had first a plain wall, then a single pilaster, and finally a group of three pilasters, we begin here in Plate VI with a single pilaster, to be followed by groups of three and groups of five.

In Gothic architecture it is customary, besides these cross-ribs and wall-ribs, to strengthen the groins by diagonal ribs; but in Classic architecture this is seldom done.

Vaults of either kind are often stilted a little, just as arches are, only more so, as is shown in Fig. 16, so that the lower part shall not be hidden by the cornice below. In this case a plinth or base may be advantageously employed, as in Fig. 17, and even a pedestal course or Attic, as in Fig. 18.

Grouped Pilasters.—Putting pilasters together in this way, three or five in a group, presents no difficulty with the Tuscan Order, in which the half pilasters may be of any convenient width or depth. But adjustments are difficult in the case of Doric Triglyphs, and in the acanthus leaves, scrolls, dentils, and modillions of the other Orders.

The triple and quintuple breaks in the outline of the piers are sometimes more numerous than are desirable in the cornice and the attic above it. In this case, the breaks may be made to terminate against the under sides of the Corona.

Arcades.—When a vaulted corridor, of either kind, is built next to the outer wall of a building, the transverse vault is often left open on that side, the outer wall being thus reduced to a series of piers, as shown in the Plates. In this case the simple square piers may be replaced by single columns (Fig. 9).

The piers with three or five pilasters on the inner side may, on the outer side, either be left plain or decorated with pilasters running the whole height of the wall, after the Roman manner.

Such open arcaded vaults are common in the cloisters of monasteries. But they are "Groined" Arches not "Cloistered" Arches.

Rooms.—Groined vaults of this kind are available, of course, for covering rooms, either square or oblong. If the length of a room is an even multiple of its width, a corresponding number of square vaults will, of course, exactly cover it (see *A*, Fig. 19). If not, the difference can be made up with sections of barrel vaults (*B*, Fig. 19). Cruciform rooms may be covered with groined arches in the same manner (*A* and *B*, Fig. 20).

Since cloistered arches are closed in at the sides by walls, a series of them form just so many different rooms, and passage through them can be had only by making openings in the separating walls. These openings, whether doorways or arches, may be of any width, even as wide as the corridor. But they have to be cut in the wall (Fig. 21). They cannot, without inconvenience, go higher than the springing line of the vault. A free passage is not, as in the case of the Groined Vault, suggested by the vault itself.

Corridors and cloisters vaulted with cloistered arches are not common. But a notable example is to be found in the upper story of the Loggia of the Vatican Palace, in which is the series of pictures called "Raffaelle's Bible" (Plate VII).

An oblong room can be covered also by the two halves of a cloistered arch, with a segment of barrel vault between them (Fig. 22). A groined arch may be used instead of a barrel vault (*B*, Fig. 19), or all three may be employed, as in Fig. 23.

Penetrations.—*Plate VIII.*—A groined vault can be lighted by windows set high up in the walls under the vaults, as in Fig. 23, and these may be made so large as to fill the whole arch. But the walls of a cloistered arch run no higher than

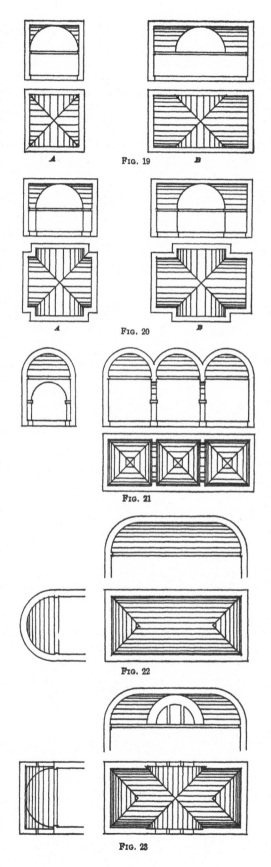

FIG. 19

FIG. 20

FIG. 21

FIG. 22

FIG. 23

the spring of the vaults, and to get windows above that level one has to resort to a transverse vault (giving a groined arch, as in Fig. 23), or to what are called *Penetrations*. These are small barrel vaults that intersect the larger ones and make a sort of partial groining.

When two cylinders of equal radius intersect one another, as in Plate IV, *A*, the line of intersection is an ellipse; but when the radii are different, the line of intersection is an irregular curve, as is shown in Plate VIII, *A*. When the penetration is made at right angles, the groin is a wavy line such as is seen in perspective at *B*. The intersecting surface has a regular geometrical character, but the line of intersection has not. But since the form of the line is more noticeable than the form of the vault, it is customary, in both Gothic and Classic Architecture, to substitute for the regular surface and irregular line of intersection a regular line and an irregular surface. In place of the wavy line shown at *B*, a broken line is used, as shown at *C*. This consists of arcs of two vertical ellipses, meeting at a point. When the planes in which they lie, are, as is usual, and as appears in the figure, taken at 45 degrees with the wall below, their projections make, in plan, a right angle. The curves are similar to the elliptical hollow groins in the corner of the vault, and their vertical projections appear as arcs of the same radius as the cylindrical vault, and look like a pointed arch.

Between these elliptic lines and the semicircular vault in the plane of the wall lies a warped or conoidal surface, which takes the place of the intersecting cylinder.

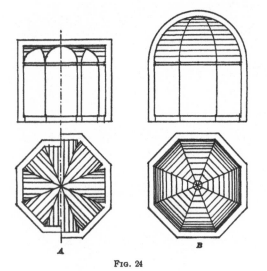

Fig. 24

If two such penetrations meet in the corner of a room, the elliptical line lies partly in a solid angle, partly in a hollow one (Plate VIII, *F*).

But if the planes in which these arcs lie, are set thus at 45 degrees with the wall, and if the elements, or generatrices, of the warped surface are right lines, the element that goes from the top of the wall arch to the point where the elliptic arcs meet will pierce the vault. A portion of the line will lie within the cylindrical surface of the vault, and the warped surface will at that point be convex down. To avoid this, the generatrices, or elements of the warped surface, must be curves, convex up, as shown in the Plate at *C*.

When rectilinear elements are used, piercing the vault may be avoided, as at *D*, by making the highest element tangent to it. The vertical planes in which the curves of intersection lie, will then make with the wall angles of less than 45 degrees, and their horizontal projections will make an obtuse angle with each other, as in the figure.

In either case, the points at the top of the penetrations are often, as at *C* and *D*, joined together by a horizontal molding, which divides the lower and steeper portion of the cloistered vault containing the penetrations from the upper portion, which is almost flat. This is called a *False Coved Ceiling*, since, although it is a true vault, the upper portion is nearly flat and it looks very much like a Coved Ceiling.

Coved Ceilings.—A flat ceiling surrounded with a cylindrical coving, is called a *Coved Ceiling* (Plate VIII, *E*). It is not a real vault, though it looks like the kind of Cloistered Arch with a horizontal molding just described. When the coving has an arc of 90 degrees, with penetrations of the same radius, the result is just half a groined arch, as appears in the figure. But the coving may have a larger radius and a smaller arc, and the penetrations may also have a smaller radius than the coving, in which case they are like those of a cloistered arch, as shown at *B, C, D,* and *E*.

Octagonal Plans.—Both Groined and Cloistered Vaults may be erected upon an octagonal plan (see Fig. 24). In this case, the height of the groined arch, as appears at *A*, instead of being half the width of the room, is only half the width of one side of the octagon, and the solid angle of the groin has the shape of a very flat ellipse. In the octagonal cloistered arch, on the other hand, as shown at *B*, the height is half the width of the room, and the hollow groins are nearly semicircular.

These octagonal vaults are often called Octagonal Domes, and are frequently somewhat pointed, as in the case of the Cathedral at Florence (Plate XII), the radius of the vaults being more than half the width of the octagon.

ROOFS

Barrel vaults and groined and cloistered arches are some-times, in Byzantine and Oriental Architecture, visible from the outside, but they play a small part in the exterior ele-vation of Classical or even of Gothic buildings, in which they are habitually covered by sloping roofs. These are generally of wood, though the vaults are sometimes loaded with masses of masonry that are brought to a recti-linear form (Fig. 25). In these cases, of course, they have to carry this weight in addition to their own, but the additional stiffness of the mass tends to prevent an increase of thrust upon the walls. Roofs of solid masonry are naturally made as light as possible, and the vaulting is carried well above the eaves, as in the figure. But wooden roofs generally lie entirely above the vaulting, the crown of which is on a level with the eaves, as shown in Fig. 26.

Gabled Roofs.—Gabled Roofs correspond in form to barrel and groined arches (Fig. 27, *A*, *C*, and *D*), and hipped roofs to cloistered arches (*B*), the valleys answering to the groins, and the hips to the hollow groins. Roofs with a flat on top correspond to Coved Ceilings, and Dormers and extra gables correspond to the different kinds of penetrations (Fig. 27 *E* and *F*).

Pyramidal Gabled Roofs.—*Plate IX.*—The intersecting gables of a roof are generally horizontal prisms, so that the ridges are level, and when the roofs are similar their point of intersection is at the same height as the peaks of the gables, as at *A*. But sometimes the ridges are sloped upwards and meet at a higher point, or apex, as at *B*, *C*, and *D*. As the apex is raised higher and higher, the horizontal cross-section, from four gables of equal height, is at first a four-pointed star, as at *B*, and finally becomes an irregular octagon, as at *D*; and there is an intermediate stage at which, as at *C*, it is a square or diamond, the line from the apex to the corner being at this stage neither a hip nor a valley. It then lies half-way between the peaks of the two gables, and, as appears from the figure, the slope of the ridge is parallel to that of the gables. The roof is a square pyramid set cornerwise. This kind of roof is common on the towers of Romanesque Churches in Germany, as is illustrated at *E*.

An elegant variation of the type shown at *C* is obtained by cutting off the corners so as to produce, in plan, an octagon of unequal sides, as in the towers of a church at Providence, R. I., as shown at *G*.

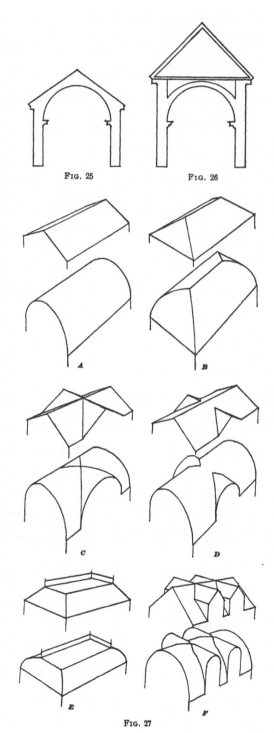

FIG. 25   FIG. 26

A   *B*

C   *D*

E   *F*

FIG. 27

When the ridges of the eight gables of an octagonal roof, like that shown in Plate IX at *H*, are sloped up to a central point, the cross-section is at first an eight-pointed star, as at *I*, and finally becomes a polygon of sixteen sides, as at *K*. Here, again, there is an intermediate stage, as appears in the figure at *J*, in which the roof has the shape of an octagonal pyramid set askew, with its sides toward the points of the gables. At this stage, the lines from the apex, or central point, to the corners are neither hips nor valleys, but lie half-way between the peaks of the gables, as in the previous example. The central point, or apex, may be found by drawing such a line.

Other Roofs.—Plate X.—Besides Hipped and Gabled Roofs, with a single slope, there are the so-called Dutch or Gambrel Roofs, or gables of two slopes, as in Plate X, *A*, and the so-called Mansard Roofs with hips in two slopes, of either a straight or a curved outline, convex or concave, with or without a flat on top. The lower pitch of such a roof is often crowned by a heavy molding or cornice, a molding or rib also decorating the hips. A cresting or railing often crowns the ridge of a roof, and the flat is generally, and naturally, surrounded with a railing, or balustrade. A truncated hipped roof, with neither an upper roof nor any sort of cresting above it, is apt to look clumsy. This is exemplified in Plate X, *C*. The lower part of the figure shows how this effect may be avoided, and the existence of the flat concealed, by means of gables.

Roofs composed of the same geometrical elements, and exactly alike in plan, may be made to vary greatly in architectural character and expression merely by changing the slope (Plate X, *D*). Variety may be obtained in the same building by using steeper roofs at one point than at another (Plate X, *E*).

Roofs of Equal Slope.—But, in general, it is most convenient, if the slope is not to vary much, not to vary it at all, adopting a uniform inclination all around, as in Plate XI. If the eaves are, as at *A*, all at the same level, the height of each roof will be proportioned to the width of the portion of the building that it covers. The valleys and hips will also be of uniform inclination, and in the plan of the roof they will, as in the figure, all lie at 45 degrees.

In laying out the plan of such a roof, it is convenient first to use only hips, finally substituting gables where they are desired. The roof may then be regarded as consisting of a principal oblong pyramid, with smaller half pyramids attached to it. The base of the principal pyramid will be the widest parallelogram that can be drawn within the outline of the building. The rest of the plan will then consist of wings, or *L*'s, and if these are added one by one, in the order of their width, the plan of the roof, however complicated with ridges, hips, and valleys, is easily constructed. Each roof is then less high than the preceding one, and is easily adjusted to it. Figs. *B* and *C* illustrate the steps of this procedure. The principal oblong pyramid is numbered I, and the successive additions to it are numbered II and III. In drawing *B*, part of the hip *a* is obliterated, as is part of the hip *b* in drawing *C*. At *D*, the same roof is treated erroneously, the narrower wing being taken up before the wider one. The wing III comes out wider than II, and consequently higher, and accordingly will not fit against it.

If the highest peak is cut off, as at *E*, a flat is obtained. If it is cut off at the level of one of the lower ridges, as in the figure, this ridge and the flat can have crestings at the same level.

It sometimes happens, as at *F*, that a building is of such a shape that a sequence of additions to the main parallelogram, each narrower than its predecessor, cannot be arranged. Whether treated as at *G* or as at *H*, wing III comes out wider than wing II. This occurs whenever, as in this case, as appears at *F*, there are two independent crests to the roof, connected by a ridge, *R*, like a mountain with two summits. It always happens then that the second wing comes out wider than the first; that is, that III is wider than II, as at *G* and *H*. In this case, two treatments are always possible, as shown at *I*, where there is a horizontal valley, *V*, instead of a horizontal ridge, as at *F*.

This alternative is distinctly presented at *J*, where the two parallelograms that compose the plan are drawn out in full. The intersecting hips and valleys form a square, or diamond, the corners of which are marked *r*, *r'*, *v*, *v'*. If the line *r r'* is taken, the roof has a horizontal ridge, as at *F*. If the line *v v'* is taken, it has a horizontal valley, as at *I*.

This procedure is of service in laying out the slight slopes of tinwork on a flat roof, so as to secure an even flow of water and avoid horizontal valleys.

DOMES

A vault erected upon a circular wall is called a *Dome*, or *Cupola*. It is built up of successive courses of horizontal rings, the horizontal joints being the continuous ones. The inner surface of a dome is sometimes a plain spherical surface; but it is sometimes enriched by vertical ribs, and sometimes by horizontal moldings, following the lines of the horizontal joints, and sometimes by both, which gives a series of trapezoidal panels, as in the Pantheon at Rome (Plate XII).

Domes are sometimes erected upon square or octagonal plans, in which the corners, which the dome does not cover, are covered by *Pendentives*. These are either diagonal arches, as shown in Fig. 28 *A*, or, more commonly, spherical triangles, as shown in Fig. 28 *B*, and also in Plates VII and XV.

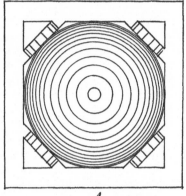

There are three kinds of domes with spherical pendentives. In the first kind, the pendentives are a portion of the same sphere as the dome they support, as at *A* and *B*, Fig. 29, and the dome is flat, or segmental, having, on a square plan, a vertical arc of only 90 degrees. In this case, it is generally separated from the pendentive by a horizontal molding, as at *A*. But this is sometimes omitted, in which case the pendentive is called *continuous*, as at *B*, and in the lower story of the Loggia of the Vatican (Plate VII).

In the second kind, the pendentive is discontinuous, the dome being generally a full hemisphere, constructed with a radius less than that of the sphere of which the pendentives form a part (see Fig. 28 *B* and Fig. 29 *C*).

In the third kind, a vertical cylinder, called a *Drum*, is erected upon the pendentives, as at *D*, and the dome rests upon that, as upon a circular wall, as in St. Peter's (Plate XII).

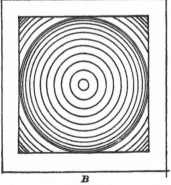

Domes are sometimes lighted by small dormer-windows, which are frequently circular; sometimes by rectangular windows in the drum, as at St. Peter's; sometimes by an eye, as in the Pantheon in Rome; or by a *lantern*, which is a cylindrical or octagonal structure resting on the summit, and nearly closing the eye. But such a lantern gives very little light.

Unless a dome is very large, the height of the drum required to make it conspicuous from without, gives an excessive height within. It is customary, accordingly, to insert a hemispherical ceiling, or second dome, at a lower

A

B

F<small>IG</small>. 28

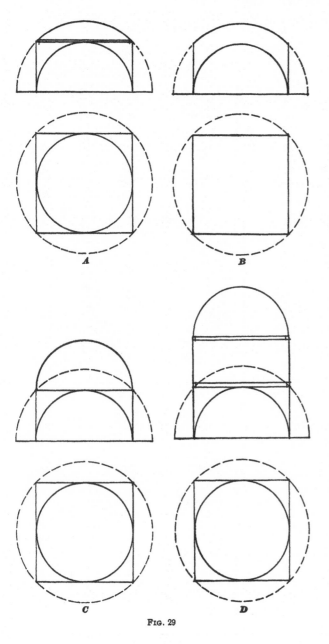

FIG. 29

point within, as is done at St. Paul's in London, in the Capitol at Washington, and in the Chapel of the Invalides in Paris (Plate XII).

Outside, as within, domes are sometimes plain, sometimes enriched with vertical ribs and with small dormers. Horizontal ribs are less common. The drums are often strengthened by buttresses, as at St. Peter's, or by circular colonnades, as in the Pantheon in Paris, or by both, as in St. Paul's Church in London (Plate XII).

Octagonal Domes.—Octagonal Domes, which are really cloistered arches, are treated in the same way. Both octagonal domes, as at Florence, and circular domes, as in Rome, London, and Paris, are frequently made more or less pointed. This gives greater height and a more graceful outline with less horizontal thrust. But it is frequently overdone.

FIG. 30

Even where there is no drum, the dome is often stilted a little within, to clear the cornice at the spring, just as is done with arches and vaults, and, as with them, a high plinth or even an attic is sometimes used.

Half Domes and *Niches*, large and small, are of frequent occurrence, both outdoors and within, where they often close the openings in the arches that support groined vaults or domes. On a small scale, they serve as receptacles for statues and busts (Plate XII). In niches, the vertical joints are sometimes made continuous, instead of the horizontal ones (Fig. 30).

DOORS AND WINDOWS

Doorways are generally about twice as high as they are wide, or, as is said, two squares high. Common doors are three or four feet wide and six or eight feet high. The opening is covered, and the wall above is supported, either by a straight beam of stone or wood, called the *Lintel*, or by an arch. But as the opening is generally closed by a *door*, in one or two valves, and it is more convenient to have this rectangular, even when an arch is employed, a lintel is often used below the arch, on a level with the Impost, to receive the door, and another horizontal beam, or *Threshold*, is put in at the bottom, so that it may fit tight and yet swing clear.

The sides of the doorway are called the *Jambs*. They are sometimes built up in courses, like the rest of the wall, and sometimes consist of a single stone (see Fig. 31). In either case, they were anciently made to slope inwards a little, so as to diminish the span of the lintel (Fig. 32). The joint around the edges of the lintel and of the jamb post is often emphasized by a raised molding, like that upon an architrave, and the lintels are sometimes, like an architrave, divided into two or three bands. This treatment is habitually carried down the jamb, which is then also commonly called an architrave. When the lintel is so long as to overrun the door posts, the projections are called *Crossettes* (see Fig. 33 *A*, *B*, *C*, and *D*). The inner band does not show a crossette. The neatest arrangement is to have the outer band with its molding just as wide as the inner band, as shown at *A*, Fig. 33. Then the crossette comes entirely on the lintel. But this is not very common, and the crossette is often cut by the joint, part of it coming upon the door post (Fig. 33 *B*). One way to avoid this is to cut out the under side of the lintel to receive the doorway, as shown at *C*, Fig. 33. What is called a *Double Crossette* is shown at *D*, in the same figure. ·

The doorway may be further enriched by adding to the architrave, the frieze, cornice, and pediment, or attic, of a full order (Fig. 34 *A* and *B*).

Still greater richness is secured by slightly lengthening the corona of the entablature, and supporting the ends upon brackets, or consoles, which come down just outside the door posts, and, in turn, often rest upon a tall, shallow strip called a *chambranle;* this is often paneled. The type of this doorway is that of the Church of San Damaso, by Vignola, in the façade of the Palace of the Cancellaria at Rome (Plate XIII, *A*).

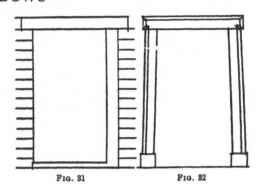

FIG. 31   FIG. 32

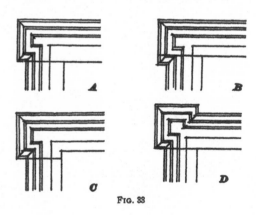

FIG. 33

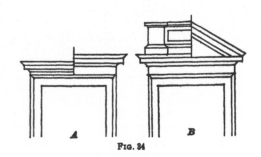

FIG. 34

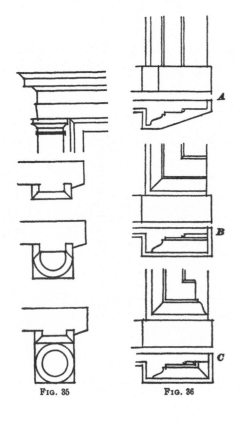

FIG. 35   FIG. 36

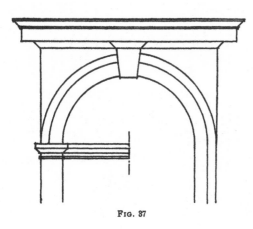

FIG. 37

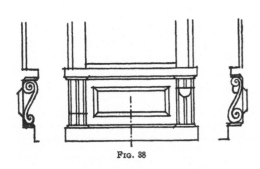

FIG. 38

But sometimes the door post is treated as a pilaster and furnished with a cap and base (Fig. 35). The molding at the top of the lintel is then not carried down at the ends, but is returned upon itself. In this case, also, a full entablature may be employed, and the treatment made still richer by setting in front of the pilaster a three-quarter column or a full column. This is often set well in front of the pilaster, so as to make a shallow porch. But in these cases, the doorway is generally furnished with an independent door jamb and lintel, as shown in the figure.

At the bottom of the door post, the moldings are sometimes received upon a block slightly beveled to conform to their outline, and whether this happens or not they are often turned inwards toward the doorway and then sometimes again returned upon themselves, as in Fig. 36, *A*, *B*, and *C*.

In Northern Italy, the cornice over a doorway, instead of carrying an angular pediment, or a curved pediment, with an arc of 90 degrees, is often surmounted by a semicircular pediment, the extrados of which extends as far as the ends of the frieze below it (Plate XIII, *B*).

Doorways with semicircular heads are generally treated like a Roman Arch (Plate XIII, *D*). But sometimes the pilasters are omitted, as in Fig. 37. The cornice then rests only upon the keystone and the spandrels. In either case, the impost is often carried across as a lintel.

Windows.—The treatment of windows differs from that of doors chiefly because a window sill is set higher from the ground than a threshold, and while a doorway is, in general, rectangular, and higher than it is wide, windows may conveniently be made of various shapes. Moreover, while doorways are in general single, and isolated, windows habitually occur in a series, more or less connected with one another. Windows also are often divided by horizontal bars, called *Transoms*, and by vertical ones, called *Mullions*.

Window Sills.—A long window, coming down to the floor, has a sill like a threshold, though thicker. But the sill is generally set two or three feet above the floor, and in that case often has a panel beneath it, and the window jamb is often supported by a console, or an inverted console (Fig. 38). But sometimes the architrave is carried across the bottom of a window, with or without crossettes at the lower corners. This is more usual when the window is square, or wider than it is high (Fig. 39).

Circular and oval windows are called *Oeils-de-Boeuf* (Fig. 40). Semicircular or segmental windows are naturally employed under arches, and are divided by radiating, or more frequently by vertical, mullions (Figs. 41 and 42). Windows that extend through several stories generally have wide paneled transoms at the floors (Fig. 43). The window sill is often continued from window to window, forming a stringcourse, with or without moldings beneath it, and a continuous pedestal often connects the panels below the window sills, forming a sort of basis upon which the separate windows stand (Fig. 44). The entablature above the windows is sometimes carried along in the same way, and in this case the enclosed rectangular wall space between the windows is often paneled (Fig. 45). But connecting the lintels without connecting the sills leaves the windows "hanging" (Fig. 46).

Sometimes, as in the Hotel de Ville at Paris, the windows are treated with a simple architrave, and the architectural embellishment of the series is bestowed entirely upon the wall spaces between them (Plate XIII, *E*).

Round-headed windows are treated in the same way as round-headed doors. But the semicircular heads are sometimes, especially in Northern Italy, occupied by a species of tracery, supported by one or two mullions. In this case, the larger semicircle is much crowded; it is usually somewhat stilted (see Plate XIV, *F*).

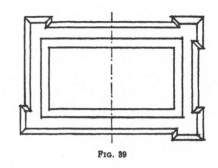

Fig. 39

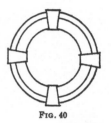

Fig. 40

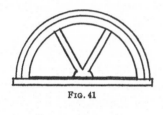

Fig. 41

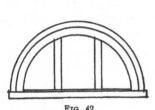

Fig. 42

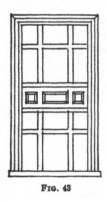

Fig. 43

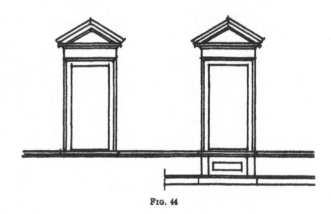

Fig. 44

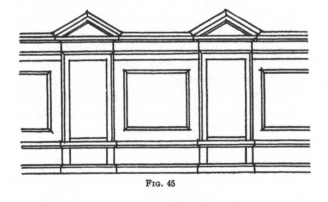

Fig. 45

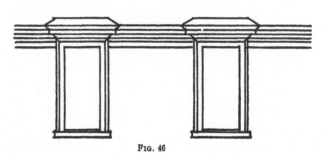

Fig. 46

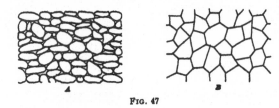

FIG. 47

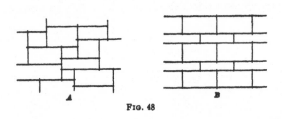

FIG. 48

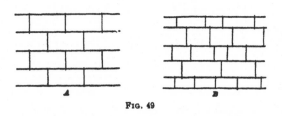

FIG. 49

WALLS

The aspect of Stone Walls differs according to the kind of masonry employed. In rubblework (Fig. 47 *A*), the size and shape of the stones and the direction of the joints are entirely a matter of accident; in "Cyclopean work" (Fig. 47 *B*), the stones are large, are of nearly uniform size, are bounded by right lines, and are carefully fitted together, but the joints run in every direction; when, as is shown in Fig. 48 *A*, the joints are horizontal and vertical, and the separate stones are of course rectangular, they are then sometimes regular in size, but laid in courses of varying height, as at *B*, Fig. 48, or of equal length, and all of the same height, as in the Roman *Opus Quadratum*, shown at *A*, Fig. 49. Sometimes the courses are alternately wide and narrow, as shown at *B*, Fig. 49.

Rustication.—In all these cases, though the jointing conspicuously affects the character of the surface, the joints hardly count as an architectural feature, unless, as is often done where the stones have a regular shape, they are emphasized by leaving the face of each stone rough, or by beveling the edges of each stone, or by cutting a chisel draft around it, the center being raised. This treatment is called *Rustication*. It is sometimes applied to the whole surface of a wall (Fig. 50), but is more frequently used in arches, where it emphasizes the separate voussoirs (Fig. 51), and upon the *quoins* at the corners of buildings (Fig. 52). But these, ordinarily, like the stones of the rest of the wall, are regarded as constituting a plane and uniform surface, as is illustrated in Fig. 3.

Quoins.—Quoins are sometimes all made of the same size (Fig. 53 *A*), sometimes alternately large and small (Fig. 53 *B*), but all square in plan. In this case, it is best to have the top one and the bottom one large, as shown. But when, as is often done, they are oblong and all of the same length, but laid with the long side first on one side and then on the other (Fig. 53 *C*), this of course cannot be secured.

When a chisel draft is used, it is best, if the stones are all of the same length, to cut it only on the ends and upper edge, as in Fig. 53 *A*, since this both protects the joint and renders it inconspicuous. But if the stones are alternately long and short, this is impracticable, as appears from Fig. 53, *B* and *C*, and the four edges must be treated alike.

The surface of the stones is sometimes left rough, retaining the quarry face. Sometimes it is cut smooth, or roughly tooled (Fig. 54 *A*); sometimes carved either with an irregular pattern, called *vermiculation*, as if worm-eaten (Fig. 54 *B*), or with decorative patterns (Fig. 54 *C*). The former is more usual on quoins, the latter, as in the Louvre and Tuileries, on the drums of columns. Sometimes this surface is pulvinated, (Fig. 54 *D*), and sometimes beveled (Fig. 54 *E*), and the alternate stones sunk (Fig. 54 *F*). In either case, a chisel drift may be added around the edges.

The vertical pile of quoins, one over another, is called a *Chain*.

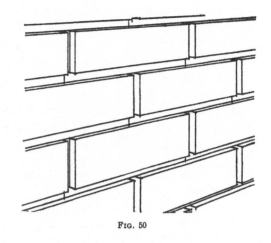

Fig. 50

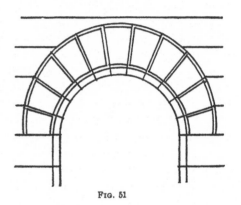

Fig. 51

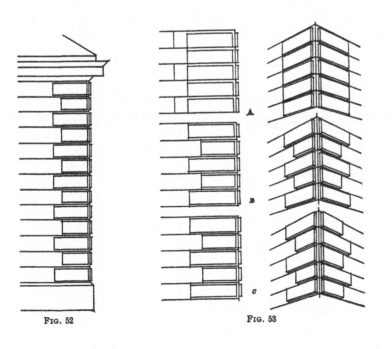

Fig. 52   Fig. 53

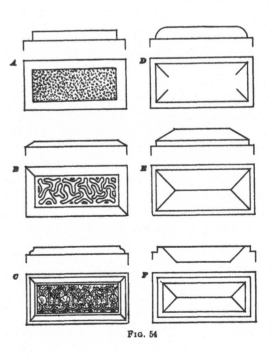

Fig. 54

Florentine Arches.—Voussoirs sometimes terminate at the extrados of the arch, as in Fig. 55 *A*, and the extrados is then sometimes made pointed, as at *B*, which is called a *Florentine Arch*, the joints sometimes meeting those of the wall, an adjustment which may have suggested this treatment (Fig. 55 *C*). But frequently the outer end of each voussoir is cut with both vertical and horizontal joints, so as to bond into the other masonry of the wall (Fig. 55 *D*). The keystone, and sometimes the two voussoirs on either side of it, is then generally made of extra length, as in the figure. Voussoirs are sometimes made angular, with a lug (Fig. 55 *E*); but this is apt to break off.

If a flat arch (Fig. 56) is built with rusticated voussoirs and the jambs are also rusticated, the beveled edges come badly together at the corners, as is seen at *A*. This may be avoided by making the *Skew Back*, as the corner stone is called, either longer (Fig. 56 *B*) or, preferably, higher (Fig. 56 *C*), or by having a chisel draft all around the stone outside the raised surface (Fig. 56 *D*).

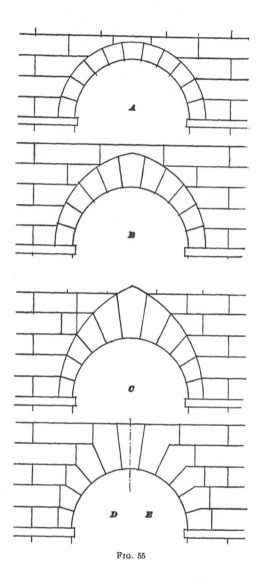

FIG. 55

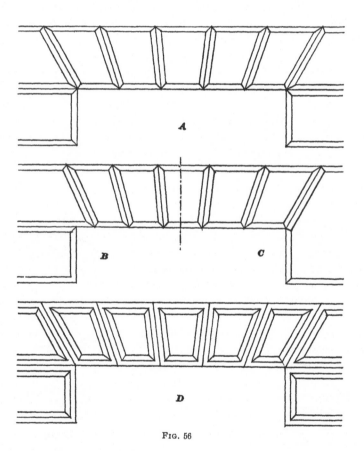

FIG. 56

WALL TREATMENT

The contrast between the richer and more broken surfaces presented by columns, entablatures, string-courses, doors, windows, and rusticated groins, and the plain wall surface that separates them, is one of the most effective elements in architectural composition, and it is enhanced by making the masonry of the wall as smooth as may be, and even concealing its natural roughness by stucco or plaster. But it is sometimes desirable on the contrary to enrich the wall surface by encrusting it with architectural details. Examples of this are shown in Plate XIV.

In Classical Architecture, as in other styles, the principal decorative details are features that were originally used for structural purposes, such as columns and entablatures, arches and piers, pediments and pedestals, doors, windows, and niches. All these things have been brought into such good form that they have a decorative interest, quite independent of their structural value. When used upon a wall, they sometimes constitute the main fabric, the wall behind them being only a screen, or *Wall veil*, carrying only its own weight. But sometimes the wall is the real structure, the architectural features being, as it were, carved upon its surface. These, in serious work, closely conform to the forms and proportions that are imposed upon real constructions by considerations of strength and stability. But being in fact only a surface decoration, they are not really bound by such restrictions, and great freedom is sometimes used, especially when the architecture is represented in paint or plaster, as at Pompeii. During the period of the Renaissance we find, not infrequently, especially in the baroque style in France and Germany, and the Churriguresque in Spain, and the Elizabethan and Jacobean periods in England, architectural forms and combinations executed in stone that would not stand up if unsupported by the wall behind them.

In the decoration of walls, pilasters, rather than columns, naturally play the chief part, sometimes accompanied by a pedestal course, or by an Attic, or by both. The wall surfaces between the pilasters are often occupied by a second and smaller order, surmounted by an entablature, or merely by a string-course. Either order may carry pediments, and the lower one may carry arches, after the manner of a Roman Arch or a Palladian Motive. The spaces remaining may then be occupied by niches, with round or square heads, with or without pediments, or by panels, with or without crossettes. Any of these may be cut through to make a door or window.

When the wall is regarded as only a thin screen, its thickness may be reduced by sinking the whole surface a little, leaving only plain horizontal and vertical strips all around, like the rails and stiles of a door. The center of the enclosed space is sometimes raised in like manner. The effect of this treatment is simpler and more elegant if no moldings are employed.

The decoration of wall surfaces with colonnades and arcades (large and small), pediments, panels, and niches, is exemplified in Plate XIV, *A* to *X*. This treatment is applied to both interior and exterior walls, bays, and pavilions.

In the first six figures, from A to F, there is at the bottom a continuous pedestal, or die, sometimes called a *Dado*, and at the top a similar feature, like an attic, resting upon a string-course, which has the shape of an entablature. Sometimes both features are employed, as here, and in the six figures of the third row, from M to R. Sometimes the attic is omitted, as in the fourth row of figures, from S to V, and sometimes both, as in Figs. W and X, and in the second row from the top, from G to L. The employment of an attic without a pedestal course is less common.

The main wall surface is sometimes left plain. Sometimes, as at A, it is decorated with panels, raised or sunk, with or without moldings. Sometimes, as in the other figures of this series, it is treated with single or coupled pilasters, which may, as in Fig. C, carry a pediment in the attic. These pilasters are sometimes, as in Fig. B, flanked by narrow strips of wall, which are continued across under the entablature, making the pilasters look as if planted upon a broad shallow pier, and making the wall surface between them look like a sunk panel. This is, as has been said above, an effective treatment. Similar piers, but narrow, like pilasters without bases or caps, with sunk panels between them, are often used without pilasters, as in the lower part of Figs. I and J.

In Fig. C, the attic is occupied by a pediment, and the dado, as in the other figures, by pedestals.

In Figs. D, E, and F, a smaller order of pilasters is interposed between the larger ones, supporting a string-course and attic, which in Fig. D is occupied by the sunk panels and plain narrow piers just described. In Fig. E, it is occupied by a pediment, and in Fig. F, by a still smaller order of pilasters with a circle or Oeil-de-Boeuf, between them, as in the front of the Opera House in Paris.

In the second row of figures, from G to L, there is neither pedestal course nor attic, and the wall is treated with arcades instead of with colonnades. In Fig. G, the arches spring from piers, and both the wall space beneath the arch and the pier itself are occupied by a round-headed panel, or niche. In Fig. H, the impost of the piers is carried along beneath the arch, and all the surfaces are decorated with panels. In Fig. I, the impost takes the form of an entablature of two members, without a frieze, and is supported by pilasters, all the surfaces being paneled. In Fig. J, there is no pier, a single pilaster carrying the arch, and in K the wall surface beneath the arch is occupied by a pediment and pilasters, a treatment equally possible when the arch is, as in Figs. G, H, and I, carried upon piers. In Fig. L, a smaller arcade, with still smaller pilasters, supports the string-course. Here, of course, the smaller impost need not be continued between the pilasters.

In the third series, from M to R, a smaller colonnade is introduced beneath the arches, as was done in the first series between the pilasters. This combination presents the familiar features of the so-called Roman Order, as used by the Romans in their Triumphal Arches, with pedestals below and an attic above, the piers being decorated with pilasters, and the impost of the arch continued between them. In Fig. M, the surface of the piers is paneled; in Fig. N, the spaces between the pilasters is occupied by narrow arches starting from the impost; in Fig. O, these smaller arches are beneath the impost line, and in Figs. P and Q, the arch space is, as in Figs. E and K, occupied by a pediment resting upon pilasters. In Fig. Q, the large pilasters that support the entablature are replaced by two smaller ones, one over the other. In Fig. R, a large arch rests upon short pilasters and has a smaller concentric arch within it, resting upon similar pilasters, all the wall spaces being paneled.

The fourth series of examples, from S to X, are based upon Palladio's Motive, as shown at S. Here the pier and impost of the regular Roman Order, as shown in Fig. M, are replaced by a small pilaster and an entablature of one or two members. Fig. U shows the form of window treatment common in Florence and Venice, which has already been illustrated in Plate XIII. This and the figures that follow are derived from Medieval precedents. Other combinations of these elements can easily be devised.

Pilasters.—When used in conjunction with columns, pilasters and piers often diminish in size from bottom to top by a gentle curve, just as the columns do. They have both Diminution and Entasis. This is the most convenient way, though the slope of the square angle seems excessive. But when they stand alone, they look better if made straight, with parallel sides; and even when used with columns, straight pilasters are preferred, in spite of the difficulties of adjustment that the difference of shape necessarily involves.

Fig. 57 A, B, and C shows two ways of treating the pilaster when coupled with a column. In Fig. 57 A, the lower diameters are the same, and since the diameter does not diminish, its upper diameter projects one-twelfth of a diameter beyond the line of the column and of the frieze above it. In Fig. 57 B, the upper diameters are of the same size and are in line with each other and with the frieze above, but the lower diameter of the column projects one-twelfth of a diameter beyond those of the pilaster. The diameter of the pilaster as seen in elevation is less than that of the column; but, when looked at diagonally, as it generally is, it looks quite as large, and a pier looks larger. The discrepancy in the plinths can be avoided by giving the moldings of the base of the pilaster more boldness, or those of the columns less, or by doing both.

In Fig. 57 *C*, the pilaster measures eleven-twelfths of a diameter, instead of either six-sixths, or five-sixths, as in *A* and *B*. This reduces the discrepancies to one twenty-fourth of a diameter, as in the figure.

Since, in the Doric Order, the triglyph over the corner column or pilaster is only half a diameter wide, a fragment of a metope one-sixth of a diameter wide regularly intervenes between it and the end of the frieze. But in the Library of St. Mark at Venice (see Fig. 58), Sansovino increased this dimension to three-eights of a diameter, or half a metope, supporting the corner by a huge pilaster, or pier, and then planted upon each outer face of this pier a shallow pilaster of the usual width, directly under the middle of the triglyph above. The pier is set back a little, so as to bring the face of this pilaster in line with the upper diameter of the adjacent column. A somewhat similar treatment is given to the Ionic order in the second story.

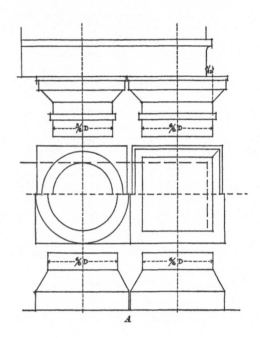

The object of this device, which has been much admired, in spite of the awkward way in which the pier is cut off at its inner corners, was to get a full half metope.

In the Cathedral at Brescia, the double corners of the piers under the central dome are occupied by Corinthian columns flanked by pilasters, the columns being on the corners. The pilasters do not diminish, while the columns do. The entablature is set in line with the face of the pilaster; but when it comes to the corner, instead of continuing in that plane, and overhanging the column, it breaks back about one-twelfth of a diameter, to the line of the upper end of the shaft. This break is carried up through the entire cornice (Plate XV).

A

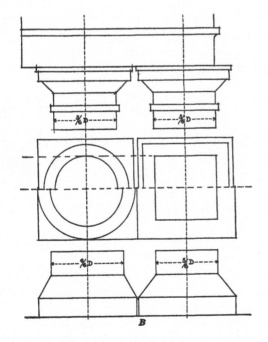

B

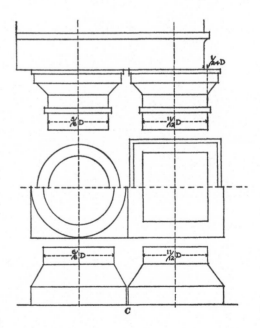

C

Fig. 57

FIG. 58

Pilasters may be placed where they mark the position of transverse walls or partitions; or at the ends of a wall, where they serve as a terminal feature in the architectural composition; or they may be set at any intermediate point where they divide the surface into well-proportioned spaces.

Pilasters of the Tuscan, Ionic, and Composite Orders can be set at any points that are, for any of these reasons, desirable ones. But in the Doric Order they must be set directly beneath a triglyph and mutule, and in the Corinthian Order it is better to have the pilasters directly beneath modillions. This means that the distance apart of Doric pilasters, on centers, must be a multiple of one and one-fourth diameters; and of Corinthian pilasters, a multiple of two-thirds of a diameter.

But coupled Doric pilasters, or columns, on account of the width of their bases, have to be set a diameter and a third on centers (see Fig. 59), the metope being made ten-twelfths of a diameter wide, or five-sixths, instead of nine-twelfths, or three-fourths, as usual. Coupled Corinthian pilasters, also, on account of the width of the capitals, cannot be less than a diameter and a half on centers (Fig. 60). The modillions between their axes are then set nine-twelfths of a diameter, or three-fourths, on centers, instead of eight-twelfths, or two-thirds, as usual. The dentils and interdentils are also increased in width by one-eighth of their own width, being one-eighth and one-sixteenth of a diameter in width, instead of one-ninth and one-eighteenth, and three-sixteenths of a diameter on centers, instead of three-eighteenths, or one-sixth, as usual.

In the Ionic Order (Fig. 61), and in Vignola's Composite Order (Fig. 62), coupled pilasters or columns present no difficulty. Their distances apart on centers is a diameter and a half, which gives room for exactly nine Ionic dentils one-sixth of a diameter on centers, or for six Composite dentils one-fourth of a diameter on centers.

External Angles or Corners.—At the end of a wall, an external angle or corner may be plain, as in Fig. 63 *A*, or it may be fortified by pilasters on each face, as in Fig. 63 *B*, *C*, and *D*. These may be united so as to form a square corner pier, as at *B*, or meet in the corner as at *C*, only the capitals uniting; or each may be set back from the corner a little way, as at *D*, so that the capitals are entirely separated. The cornice generally breaks around the angles thus formed, but the architrave and frieze often do not, as in the figure. Sometimes, as at *E*, only the bed-mold of the cornice breaks, the corona being carried along without interruption and receiving the broken bed-mold under its soffit. But unless the projection of the pilasters is exceptionally small, this gives the corona an excessive prominence when seen across the corner, as is shown at *F*.

The architrave generally overhangs the wall by the depth of the pilaster, but sometimes, especially when the pilasters

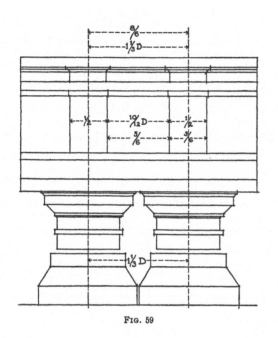

Fig. 59

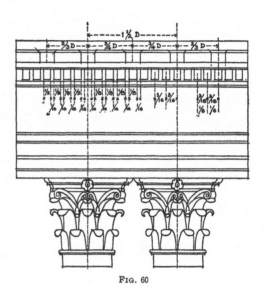

Fig. 60

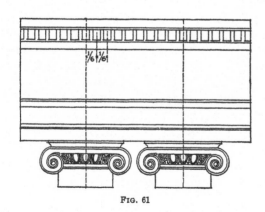

Fig. 61

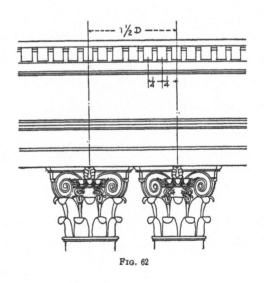

Fig. 62

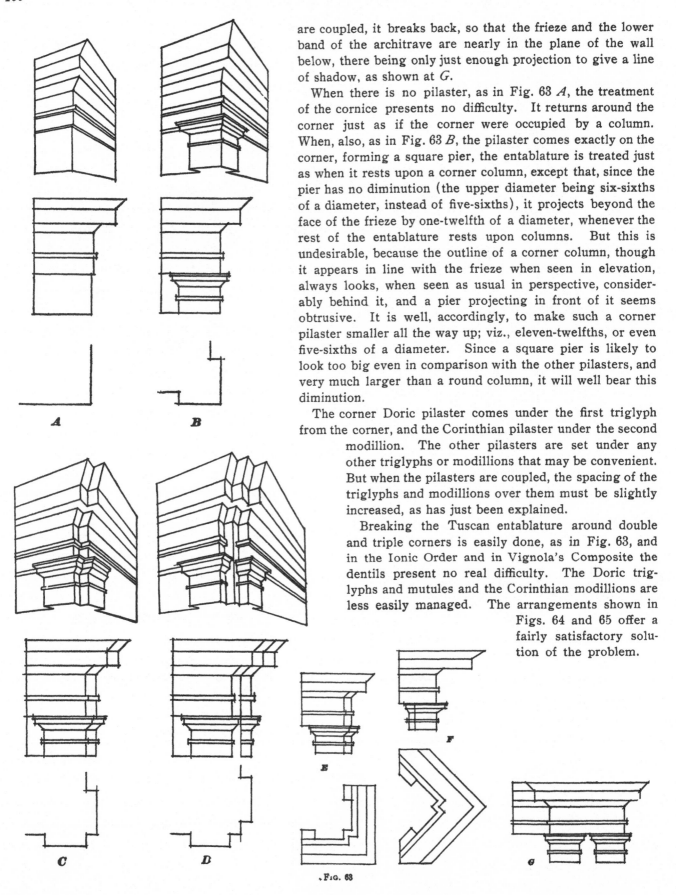

are coupled, it breaks back, so that the frieze and the lower band of the architrave are nearly in the plane of the wall below, there being only just enough projection to give a line of shadow, as shown at *G*.

When there is no pilaster, as in Fig. 63 *A*, the treatment of the cornice presents no difficulty. It returns around the corner just as if the corner were occupied by a column. When, also, as in Fig. 63 *B*, the pilaster comes exactly on the corner, forming a square pier, the entablature is treated just as when it rests upon a corner column, except that, since the pier has no diminution (the upper diameter being six-sixths of a diameter, instead of five-sixths), it projects beyond the face of the frieze by one-twelfth of a diameter, whenever the rest of the entablature rests upon columns. But this is undesirable, because the outline of a corner column, though it appears in line with the frieze when seen in elevation, always looks, when seen as usual in perspective, considerably behind it, and a pier projecting in front of it seems obtrusive. It is well, accordingly, to make such a corner pilaster smaller all the way up; viz., eleven-twelfths, or even five-sixths of a diameter. Since a square pier is likely to look too big even in comparison with the other pilasters, and very much larger than a round column, it will well bear this diminution.

The corner Doric pilaster comes under the first triglyph from the corner, and the Corinthian pilaster under the second modillion. The other pilasters are set under any other triglyphs or modillions that may be convenient. But when the pilasters are coupled, the spacing of the triglyphs and modillions over them must be slightly increased, as has just been explained.

Breaking the Tuscan entablature around double and triple corners is easily done, as in Fig. 63, and in the Ionic Order and in Vignola's Composite the dentils present no real difficulty. The Doric triglyphs and mutules and the Corinthian modillions are less easily managed. The arrangements shown in Figs. 64 and 65 offer a fairly satisfactory solution of the problem.

A   *B*

C   *D*   *E*   *F*   *G*

Fig. 63

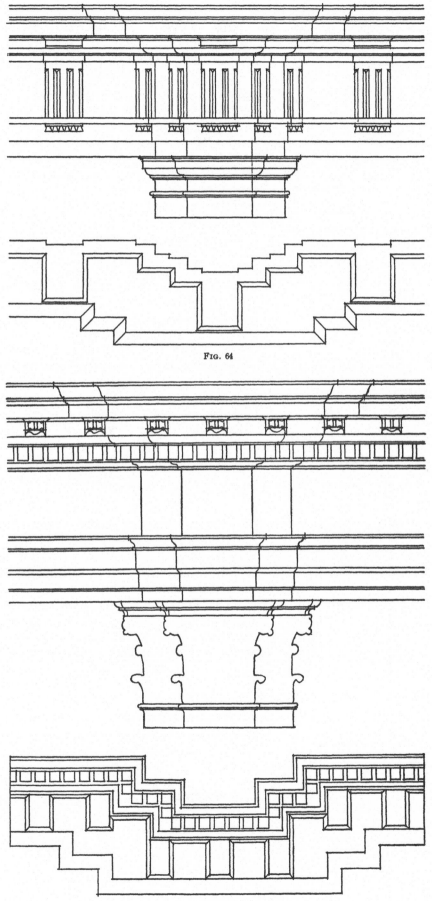

FIG. 64

FIG. 65

When the entablature breaks back from the plane of the pilaster to the plane of the wall, the problem resembles that presented by external corners, and admits of analogous solutions.

Internal Corners or Reentering Angles.—Pilasters.—In an internal corner, as in an external one, there are several ways of arranging pilasters. In Fig. 66 *A*, the entablature simply crowns the wall without any other support. In this case, the frieze generally lies nearly in the plane of the wall below. At *B*, there is a single pilaster on each wall; at *C*, a quarter pilaster is added in the corner, giving a pilaster and a quarter pilaster on each wall, the depth of the pilaster being generally a quarter of its width; at *D*, the quarter pilaster is replaced by two half pilasters, giving a pilaster and a half on each wall, but here a larger or smaller fraction may be used. In both *C* and *D*, the whole pilaster is coupled with the fragment in the corner.

As in the case of external corners, the entablature does not generally break around the outer pilaster, and unless the pilaster is deeper than usual, the soffit overhangs so little that a sufficient support is afforded by the wall beneath.

In internal corners, as of a room or of a courtyard, care must be taken that the mutules, or modillions, of the two cornices that meet at the reentering angle do not crowd upon or interfere with each other.

The Tuscan Order having none of these details presents no difficulty. Dentils, where they occur (Fig. 67), sometimes have a square interdentil in the corner, flanked by a dentil on each wall, as at *A*, an arrangement that presents, in elevation, the aspect of a double dentil, such as regularly occurs on an external angle. Sometimes a square dentil occupies the corner, as at *B*, and sometimes it is convenient to employ an L-shaped dentil, as at *C*.

Double Corners.—The Mutulary Doric.—Fig. 68 *A* shows a wall surmounted by two entablatures of Vignola's Mutulary Doric Order, meeting on an external angle, and a third entablature forming an internal angle with one of them, so that the corners of the mutules just touch. Since the outer face of each mutule is three-fourths of a diameter distant from the wall behind it, the side of each must be just three-fourths of a diameter from the adjacent wall; and as the mutules are half a diameter wide, the axis of each mutule, and consequently the axis of the triglyph and pilaster beneath it, is just one diameter from the face of the adjacent wall. It follows that, in an internal angle, the edge of a pilaster must be set at least half a diameter from the face of the adjacent frieze, or else the mutules will interfere.

If the mutules are set so far from the adjacent walls that even the little cymatia that crown them do not intersect, then these three dimensions are increased by about one-eighth of a diameter, as in Fig. 68 *B*, and the axis of the pilaster is set about nine-eighths of a diameter from the

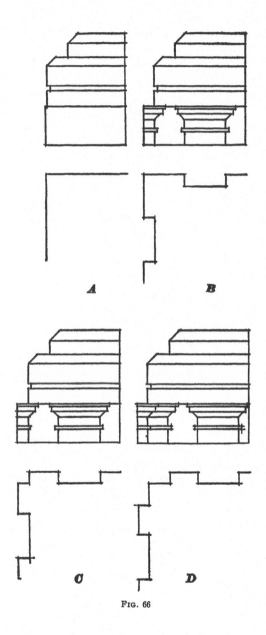

FIG. 66

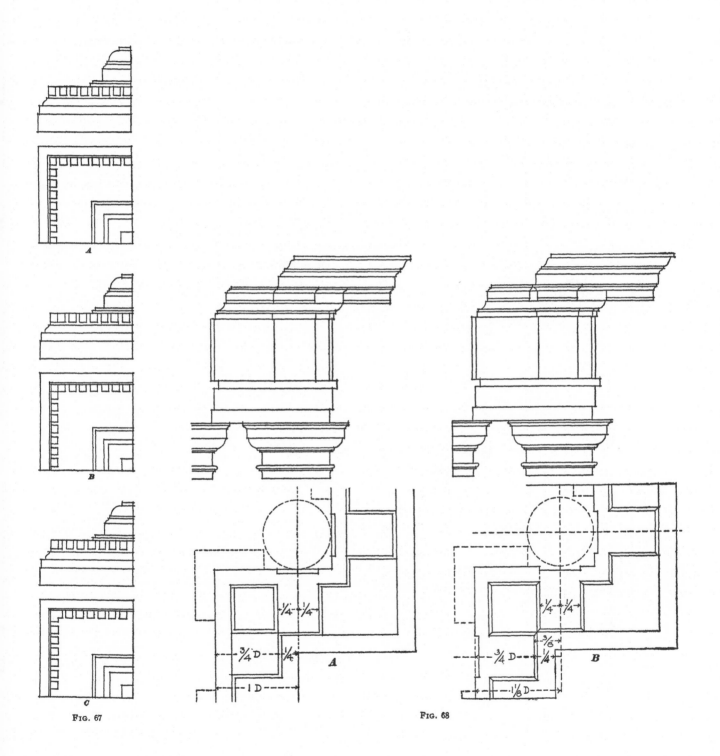

Fig. 68

adjacent wall. In the diagram, the panel in the soffit of the cornice, between the mutules, is square. If the mutules were set farther from the corner, the panel would be **L**-shaped.

The Denticulated Doric.—When, in an internal angle, two mutules of the Denticulated Doric touch at their corners, the face of one mutule and the side of the other are distant two-thirds of a diameter from the frieze behind it, or from the face of the pilaster that supports it. Since the mutule is half a diameter, or six-twelfths, wide, its axis, as well as the axis of the pilaster, is in this case distant eleven-twelfths of a diameter from the adjacent wall. The edge of the pilaster must then be set at least five-twelfths of a diameter from the adjacent frieze, or else the mutules will interfere (Fig. 69).

The Corinthian Order.—Fig. 70 shows in like manner, *A*, and *B*, external and internal angles formed by the meeting of three Corinthian entablatures. It is necessary that the modillions should be set far enough from the reentering angle not to interfere with each other.

At *A*, the axis of the second modillion from the corner is just one diameter from the face of the adjacent wall, and is accordingly just in line with the edge of the adjacent cornice. The length of the intermediate wall returning at right angles to the others is thus a Diameter and five-twelfths; or, if the pilaster is full width at the top, a Diameter and a half. At *B*, the length of this return is reduced to eight-ninths of a Diameter, and at *C* to two-ninths, or just the width of a modillion. But this pinches the dentils a little and it is better to make the return a little longer than to omit the modillion altogether. At *D*, the break is reduced to one-ninth of a Diameter, or just the width of a dentil. Fig. 68 *A* and *B* shows how walls with pilasters may be substituted for plain walls in the Doric Orders. The same substitution can be made with the Corinthian Order in Fig. 70 *A*.

Columns.—On walls, exterior or interior, columns or three-quarter columns may be used instead of pilasters as decorative features. Half columns are less available, since they have a meager appearance, are awkwardly cut across by horizontal moldings or string-courses, and look smaller than they really are. Three-quarter columns are awkwardly cut by the wall behind them, against which they stand, being more detached from it at the top than at the bottom, and, besides, they have no definite structural significance. They seem too substantial for a merely decorative feature and yet have not, as a full column seems to have, any work to do independently of the wall to which they are attached. The most satisfactory way is to regard them as the main support of the entablature and the wall above it, and to treat the wall behind them as merely a light screen, only strong enough to carry its own weight and a shallow kind of ornamentation. Three-quarter columns are, however, at best an unsatisfactory feature and a clumsy one, though from time to time much in vogue.

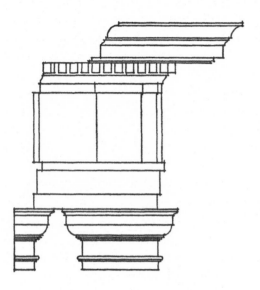

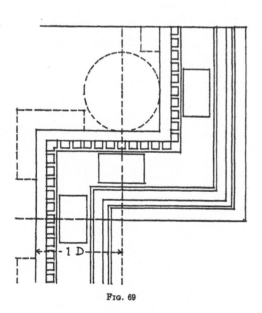

FIG. 69

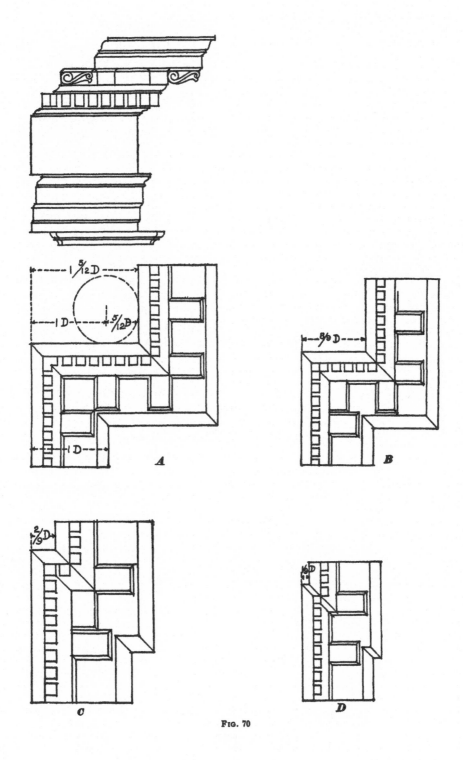

FIG. 70

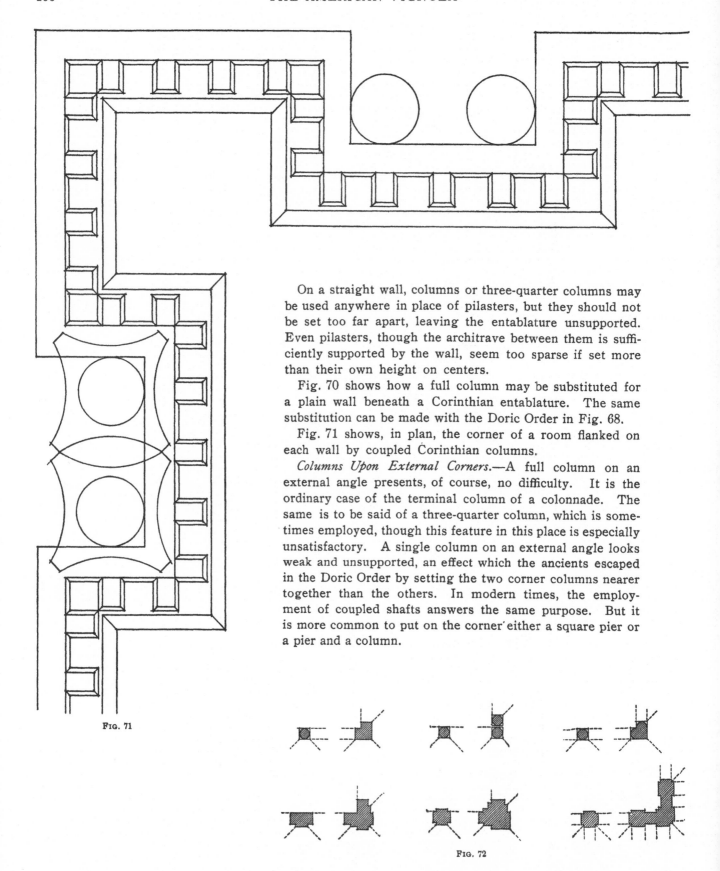

FIG. 71

On a straight wall, columns or three-quarter columns may be used anywhere in place of pilasters, but they should not be set too far apart, leaving the entablature unsupported. Even pilasters, though the architrave between them is sufficiently supported by the wall, seem too sparse if set more than their own height on centers.

Fig. 70 shows how a full column may be substituted for a plain wall beneath a Corinthian entablature. The same substitution can be made with the Doric Order in Fig. 68.

Fig. 71 shows, in plan, the corner of a room flanked on each wall by coupled Corinthian columns.

Columns Upon External Corners.—A full column on an external angle presents, of course, no difficulty. It is the ordinary case of the terminal column of a colonnade. The same is to be said of a three-quarter column, which is sometimes employed, though this feature in this place is especially unsatisfactory. A single column on an external angle looks weak and unsupported, an effect which the ancients escaped in the Doric Order by setting the two corner columns nearer together than the others. In modern times, the employment of coupled shafts answers the same purpose. But it is more common to put on the corner either a square pier or a pier and a column.

FIG. 72

Columns Upon Internal Corners.—In internal angles, in the same way, a pier, or a pier and a shaft, are commonly used instead of a single column or a group of three columns. The treatment of corners of Arcades is illustrated in Fig. 72 by examples taken from Letaronilly's *Edifices de Rome Moderne.*

Obtuse Angles.—The external angles of octagonal and hexagonal buildings are susceptible of very much the same treatment as square corners. As with the square corners, the result is controlled in the Doric and Corinthian Orders by the arrangement of the mutules and modillions. These must be laid out in such a way that the trapezoidal spaces opposite the angle shall be of as good shape and size as the conditions permit, and the pilasters, if there are any, adjusted accordingly.

Cornices.—The wall and ceiling meet at the cornice, where a series of moldings effects the transition from the vertical to the horizontal surface (Figs. 73, 74, and 75). The simplest way is by means of a large hollow coving, or inverted Scotia, with moldings above and below. If the room is a low one, its apparent height may be increased by putting this more upon the ceiling than on the wall, and vice versa. But it is quite as common to fill the angle with some kind of classical cornice, in which the depth of the corona is frequently diminished or entirely suppressed, and the sinkage on its soffit somewhat exaggerated, so that the soffit is in the same plane with the ceiling, the cymatium appearing as a molding upon it (Fig. 76). When the wall carries pilasters, the cornice has to be supported by a frieze and architrave. In this case, the suppression of the corona or the employment of a coving is hardly admissible.

Ceilings.—Ceilings, whether flat, coved, groined, or cloistered, with or without penetrations, afford an inviting field for decorative treatment, whether by painting or by architectural embellishment, since they are in plain sight, with nothing, in general, to obstruct the view. The only constructive features available for the decoration of ceilings are beams and panels.

Flat Ceilings.—*Plate XVI.* Flat ceilings occur on the under side of floors built with horizontal beams. These beams are sometimes exposed and decoratively treated with panels or caissons, carved or painted, as shown at *A* and *B.*

Fig. *A* is taken from Reynaud's *Traité d'Architecture.*

Fig. *B* shows a part of the wooden ceiling of the Basilica of Santa Maria Maggiore in Rome. It does not show the beams actually used to support the ceiling, but consists of a series of coffers or caissons made in imitation of two sets of girders equally spaced, and intersecting at right angles.

Fig. *C* exhibits a similar ceiling in the Farnese Palace in Rome. But here the decorative element is predominant, the construction suggested being an unreasonable and almost an impossible one. In ceilings of this sort the wooden panels are generally painted with decorative figures.

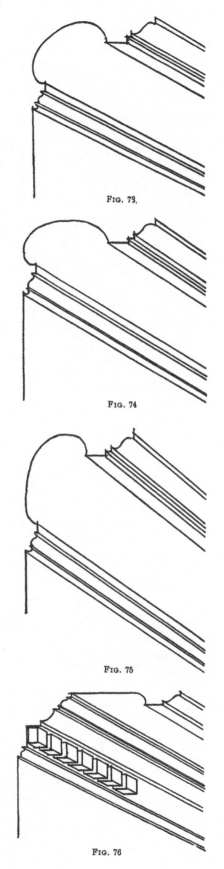

FIG. 73.

FIG. 74

FIG. 75

FIG. 76

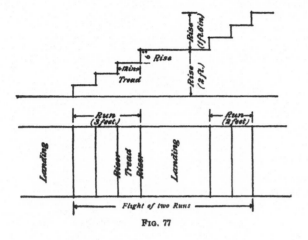

FIG. 77

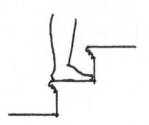

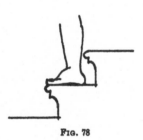

FIG. 78

Fig. *D* shows a part of the ceiling of the Sala Dello Scrutinio in the Ducal Palace in Venice. The panels are filled with pictures painted on canvas, and the moldings that enclose them are carved and gilded like picture frames, and make no pretence of filling any constructive function. This drawing is copied from one of the plates in Zanotto's work upon the Ducal Palace.

Figs. *E* and *F* represent ceilings of plaster and stucco, in which the decorative forms employed are suggested by the nature of those materials. In *E*, which is taken from the building in Bristol called the Red Lodge, these forms consist of a network of intersecting moldings, such as are common in Elizabethan work. Fig. *F* is from a ceiling in Chesterfield House, by Sir Christopher Wren, in the style of Louis XIV.

The plaster surface is often left perfectly smooth, and painted either with ornamental patterns or with pictures. But pictures on a ceiling, though always in plain sight, are difficult to see with comfort, and are apt to look upside down.

The methods used to decorate vaults and domes are similar to those used upon ceilings.

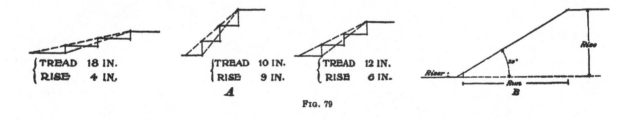

FIG. 79

STEPS AND STAIRCASES

The vertical face of a step is called a *Riser;* the flat part, where the foot rests, the *Tread.* The height of the riser is called the *Rise,* and the width the *Tread.* The total length of the steps, as one goes up, is called the *Run,* and the total height, from level to level, the *Rise.* Rise and tread are thus used in two senses. Rise means either the height of each single step, or the total height of all the steps together; tread means either the top of a step or its width. A resting place half-way up a flight of steps, is called a *Landing,* and the same term is used for the level space at the top of the flight, as well as for that at the bottom (see Fig. 77).

The rise and tread of steps may conveniently be about 6 and 12 inches, respectively. This makes the total Rise about half the Run, and the slope should not be steeper than this. Even 4 inches by 18 inches is not too flat out of doors.

Indoors, stairs may be steeper, and may even be as steep as 7 or 8 inches for the rise and 11 or 10 inches for the tread, without much inconvenience. It follows that the product of the rise and tread, when taken in inches, should be between 70 and 80.

The number of treads is, of course, one less than that of the risers.

Nosings.—The tread is often, especially when narrow, as in steep stairs, made wider than the figured dimensions indicate, overhanging the riser and overlapping the tread beneath. This projection is called a *Nosing* (Fig. 78). It gives more room for the toe in going up stairs, and for the heel in coming down, without diminishing the slope or lengthening the run.

The rise and tread give the true slope of the steps, the Rise and Run giving too steep a slope, as is shown by the dotted lines in Fig. 79 *A.* This is recognized, in sketching the side elevation of a flight of steps, by indicating a single riser at the bottom, as in Fig. 79 *B.* In such preliminary sketches, it is best to make the Run about twice the Rise, as has been said. But a slope of 30 degrees, as in Fig. 79 *B,* is a safe one for such sketches, whether outdoors or indoors. It gives treads and risers of 12 and $6\frac{1}{2}$ inches, or of 11 and 6 inches, very nearly.

When steps come to be accurately figured, the rise of each step has to be expressed in inches and fractions of an inch, since the number of the steps must be a whole number, and the height of each step is the quotient obtained by dividing the total Rise, from landing to landing, by this number. The total Rise being given, say, as 14 feet 6 inches, it is convenient to work out a Table containing the other data, as follows, assuming the rise as 7 or 6 inches and some fraction, and assuming the tread to be exactly $10\frac{1}{2}$, 10, or 11 inches; the Run then comes out as $20\frac{1}{8}$ feet, $18\frac{1}{3}$ feet, or $24\frac{3}{4}$ feet, respectively.

$$\left\{\begin{array}{l}\text{Rise} = 14'\,6'' = 174''. \qquad 7'' + \tfrac{6}{24}. \qquad 7\tfrac{1}{4}'' = \text{rise.} \\[1em] \qquad\qquad 24 = \text{No. of risers} \\ \qquad\qquad 23 = \text{No. of treads} \\[1em] \text{Run} = 20'\,1\tfrac{1}{2}'' = 241\tfrac{1}{2} = 23 \times 10\tfrac{1}{2}''. \quad 10\tfrac{1}{2}'' = \text{tread.} \end{array}\right\} \quad \left\{\begin{array}{l}\text{If 7 goes into 174, 24 times and 6 over, 24 will} \\ \text{go into 174, 7 times and 6 over.}\end{array}\right.$$

If a steeper flight were considered allowable, the table would be as follows:

$$\left\{\begin{array}{l}\text{Rise} = 14'\,6'' = 174''. \qquad 7'' + \tfrac{13}{23}. \qquad 7\tfrac{13}{23}'' = \text{rise.} \\[1em] \qquad\qquad 23 = \text{No. of risers} \\ \qquad\qquad 22 = \text{No. of treads} \\[1em] \text{Run} = 18'\,4'' = 220'' = 22 \times 10''. \qquad 10'' = \text{tread.}\end{array}\right\} \quad \left\{\begin{array}{l}\text{If 7 goes into 174, 23 times and 13 over, 23} \\ \text{will go into 176, 7 times and 13 over.}\end{array}\right.$$

If a gentler slope is desired, the table comes out thus:

$$\left\{\begin{array}{l}\text{Rise} = 14'\,6'' = 174''. \qquad 6'' + \tfrac{6}{28}. \qquad 6\tfrac{3}{14}'' = \text{rise.} \\[1em] \qquad\qquad 28 = \text{No. of risers} \\ \qquad\qquad 27 = \text{No. of treads} \\[1em] \text{Run} = 24'\,9'' = 297'' = 27 \times 11''. \qquad 11'' = \text{tread.}\end{array}\right\} \quad \left\{\begin{array}{l}\text{If 6 goes into 174, 28 times and 6 over, 28} \\ \text{will go into 164, 6 times and 6 over.}\end{array}\right.$$

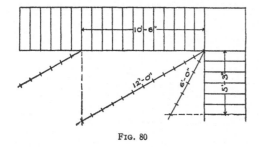

FIG. 80

It thus appears that a slight diminution in the width of the tread makes a good deal of difference in the length of the Run, that is to say, in the space on the ground required for the flight, which is often an important consideration. The same result is reached by slightly increasing the height of the risers, and thus diminishing their number and the number of treads.

If the width of the tread, in inches, is known, or assumed, it is plain that twelve treads will occupy as many feet as there are inches to the tread. This makes it easy to lay out, in plan, at any given scale, a run of twelve treads, or, by halving or doubling this dimension, a run of six treads, or of twenty-four. The position of the risers and the width of the treads may then be laid off by using a scale of twelve, twenty-four, or six, equal parts. Fig. 80 shows how two runs, one of eighteen treads and one of six, can be thus laid off by the aid of a rule showing 12 feet at the required scale, the treads being $10\frac{1}{2}$ inches wide. This is useful, in first sketches, to find out how much room on the ground a stairway will take up.

Fig. 81 *A*, *B*, and *C* shows a plan and section of a flight of five steps, in one run, with a sloping parapet on each side. At the top and bottom of the run are pedestals or posts. These posts are of the same height as the parapet, and have similar caps and bases.

At *A*, the caps and bases are shown as continuous, the sloping members being at the same height from the edge of the step that the horizontal members are from the ground, and making a slight angle at the top and bottom, so that the moldings may miter. As a result of this, the run of the rail and base, as shown at *R'*, is longer than the run of the steps, as seen at *R*, by the width of one tread and the space required for these angles. The space required for the parapet and the two posts together is greater still, as shown at *R''*, by twice the width of a post. As this is rather an awkward arrangement, making the lower landing very wide, especially when the lower rail turns at right angles, as in the figure, it is usual to set the steps farther out, as shown by the dotted lines. This increases the length of the upper landing, and diminishes that of the lower one, by half the width of a step; but it also makes the height of the sloping rail, measured from the edge of the step, less than that of a horizontal rail, by half the height of a step. Either method may be adopted when there are no posts and the rail is continuous.

But when the parapet is not continued beyond the lower post, the post is often set up on the first or second steps, which are in that case generally made wider and broader, to serve as a base to it, and sometimes curled around it, in what is called a *Curtail*, as in Fig. 81 *B*.

It is customary, in order to save room, not only to set back the lower post upon the lower step, but also to set forwards the upper post, thus bringing the two posts still

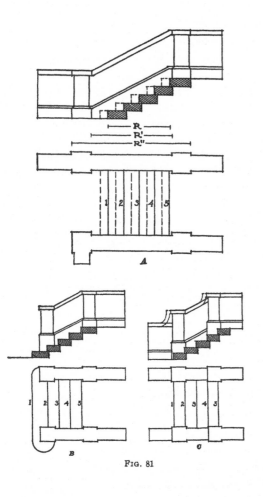

FIG. 81

nearer together, as in Fig. 81 *C*. It is not then necessary to lower the height of the sloping rail, but the plinths are lengthened and the bases run into them. The rails then either run into the dies of the pedestals, as in the figure, or rise with a sharp curve, called a *Ramp*, to the level of their caps, as shown by the dotted lines.

The sloping parapet sometimes rests upon a sloping base, called a *String*, as in the upper run shown in Fig. 83 *B*. Sometimes, as in Fig. 83 *A* and *C*, it rests upon the steps, the ends of which show beyond it. A *Balustrade*, as in Plate XVII, is often used in place of a parapet, the balustrade resting sometimes upon a continuous string, as in the Plate, sometimes on the steps themselves. When two balusters come upon the same steps, the upper one is longer than the lower one by half the height of the riser. In stone balusters this difference is generally gained by making the plinth higher. But in wooden balusters the additional height is often put into the sleeve.

Flights of Two and of Three Runs. Fig. 82 *A*, *B*, and *C* shows flights of steps in two runs, at right angles to one another. If the rails are continuous, as at *A*, the landing between the runs is **L**-shaped, since it is both at the top of the first run and at the bottom of the second. The same thing happens when there is no post, as at *B*.

If the post is moved so as to give a square landing, the rails are discontinuous and the post is twice lengthened, once because it is at the top of the lower run and

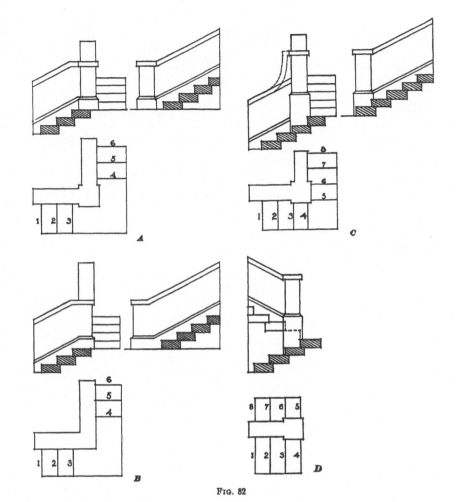

FIG. 82

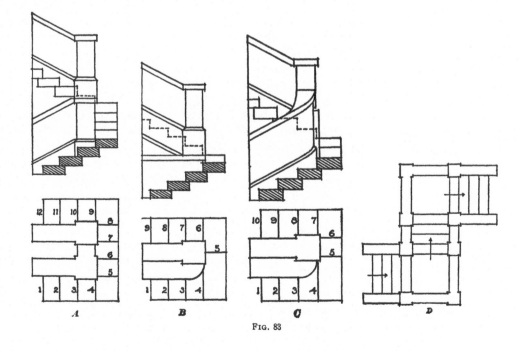

FIG. 83

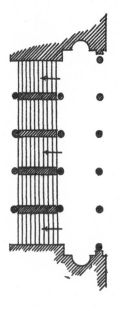

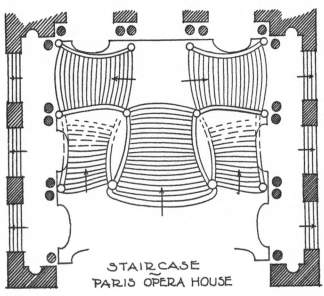

STAIRCASE
PARIS OPERA HOUSE

FIG. 84

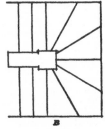

FIG. 85

once because it is at the bottom of the upper one, as appears at *C*. If the second run is parallel to the first one, as in Fig. 82 *D*, the same thing happens; but in this case the rail of the lower run is generally omitted, as in the figure.

When, in a flight of three runs, the second run consists of three or four steps, as in Fig. 83 *A*, there is room for two posts, and no new conditions are encountered; but when the second run consists of only one or two steps, the rail of the lower run is sometimes omitted and carried along a sort of horizontal shelf, as at Fig. 83 *B*. It is then best to have only one post, as in these figures. When the lower rail is not omitted, it is sometimes turned sidewise into the die of the post, as in Fig. 83 *C*. It is awkward to give this twist to a ramp.

In a flight of three runs, the second run should either be so short that, as in these examples, there is no open space between the two runs, or so long that this space is a wide one. A narrow pocket is to be avoided.

The third run may either reverse the direction of the first one, as in the previous figures, or continue it, as in Fig. 83 *D*.

In all these cases, the right lines of the steps may be replaced by curved lines, as in the Opera House at Paris (Fig. 84), the axis of the runs being still rectilinear.

Winders.—It is a saving of room to replace the square landing beween two runs by triangular steps, as in Fig. 85 *A*. Three is the best number, for if there are only two the treads are somewhat broader than those in the straight runs; and if there are more than three, they are narrower; in either case the change is undesirable. Besides, it is so much the custom to have three winders, if any, that any other number is disconcerting. The extra steps, of course, make the plinth of the post higher than it would otherwise be, by the height of two risers, as in the figure.

When the second run returns upon the first, as in Fig. 85 *B*, bringing six winders together, the length of the plinth is increased by the height of the five risers.

Circular Steps.—The axis of the runs is sometimes itself a curved line, being laid out on a circular or elliptic arc, as in Plate XVII, *A* and *B*. If the radius of the inner curve is about half that of the outer curve, there will not be too much difference in the width of the treads at the two ends, and the slope will at no part be much too steep or too flat. The rise and tread are then laid off upon a *Line of Tread*, at a convenient distance from the inner rail, generally about 18 inches. This distance may, however, be greater when the inner radius is large.

A circular flight of steps with no wall under the inner string and rail is called a *Geometrical Staircase*.

Circular steps of all these kinds are used outdoors, both as approaches to buildings and as architectural features in gardens.

In circular steps, the lines of the rails and strings are all spirals, which in elevation are projected as *Sine Curves*. These are curves of contrary flexure which, at their points of least slope, where they are parallel to the plane of projection, show the true inclination of the rails and strings (Plate XVII). The slope is, of course, much steeper for the inner rail than for the outer one. The obtuse angle at the top of the flight, where the sloping rail joins the horizontal one, is here, as elsewhere, often replaced by a ramp.

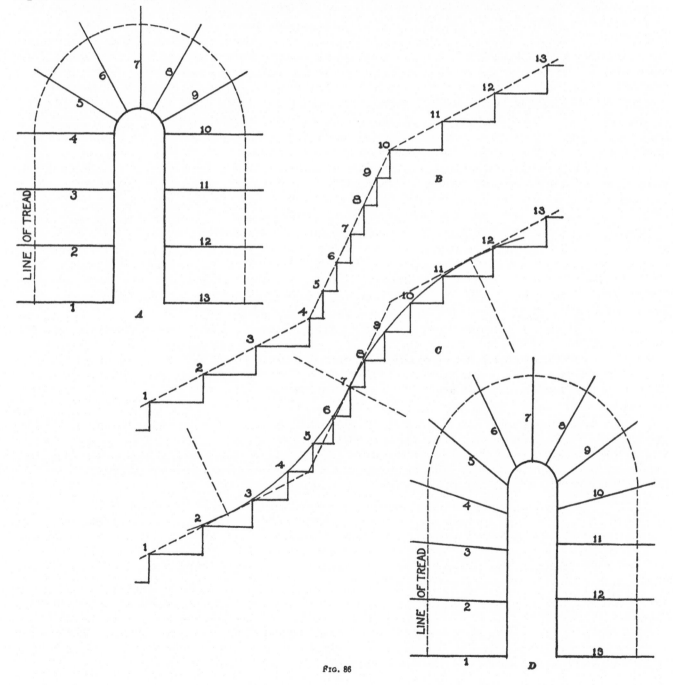

FIG. 86

Balancing.—When, as in Fig. 86 *A*, a flight of steps consists of a circular run between two straight ones, although there is no change of slope upon the line of tread, there is at the outer end of the steps a sudden change to a flatter slope, and at the inner end to a steeper one, as appears at *B*, where the inner string, with the ends of the risers and treads, is developed. The hand rail over it also makes two obtuse angles. It is practicable to avoid this awkwardness by what is called *Balancing*, or *Dancing*. For the broken line at *B* is substituted a curve of contrary flexure, as at *C*, consisting of two arcs of circles tangent to one another and to the broken line. The risers and treads at the inner ends of the steps are then redrawn to meet this curve. The width of the treads, instead of changing suddenly, now changes gradually from their greatest width to their least, and then gradually back again. The widths of the treads at their inner ends, thus ascertained, are then laid off upon the plan, as at *D*; and from the new positions of the ends of the risers, the risers themselves are drawn, as shown, through these points and the points originally taken upon the line of tread. The plan at *A* gives the broken line at *B*; the curved line at *C* gives, inversely, the plan at *D*.

Elliptic Steps.—Since concentric ellipses, though they may be equidistant along their axes, are somewhat nearer together at their haunches, it is not desirable to have true ellipses at both ends of the steps. If the inner curve is a semi-ellipse, the outer curve should be a semi-oval drawn equidistant from it. But it is more common, and easier, to substitute, in both cases, a three- or four-centered curve, as in Fig. 87 *A*, *B*, and *C*.

Equal distances being laid off upon a line of tread, the radiating lines of the risers may either be drawn to the center, as at *A*, or taken at right angles to the two curves, as at *B*. The first method gives excessively acute angles at the inner end of the steps; the other gives very wide treads near the ends of the ellipse, and a very gradual slope at their outer ends. But if these come at the top and bottom of the flight, as they generally do, this is no great disadvantage. It is customary to have wide steps at least at the bottom of a flight. But it is more usual to disregard the line of tread, and to divide both curves into an equal number of parts, drawing the lines of the risers between the points thus found, as at *C*.

Fig. 88 *A* shows how such a semi-oval can be drawn from three centers. (1) Lay off from the center *O* the semi-axes *O A* and *O B*, and then from one extremity of the major axis lay off the length of the semi-minor axis, to the point *D*. From the point thus obtained, draw a line at 45 degrees until it touches the minor axis, and from the same point lay off half the length of this diagonal line backwards along the major axis, to the point *C'*. This point is one of the desired centers. (2) A second diagonal line, drawn at right angles to the first one through the point *C'*, will cut the minor axis at the point *C''*, which is another of the desired centers. The third one, *C'''*, will be symmetrical with the first on the major axis.

This method does not work well when, as in the smaller oval shown in Fig. 87, the minor axis is less than two-thirds of the major axis.

Fig. 88 *B* shows how such a semi-oval can be drawn from five centers. (1) Taking the point *O* as the center of the required oval, draw the parallelogram *O A H B*, *O A* and *B H* being the length of the semi-major axis, and *O B* and *A H* of the semi-minor axis. (2) Draw *A B* and *H C' C''* perpendicular to it. *C'* and *C''*, and *C'''* symmetrical with *C'* are three of the required centers. (3) Taking *O D* equal to *O B*, describe upon *A D* as a diameter the semicircle *A E G D*, *E* being at the summit of the arc, and find *F* upon the vertical radius. (4) Take *O P* equal to *E F*. (5) Taking *C''* as a center, draw an arc with a radius *C'' P*, and cut it by two arcs drawn with the points *A* and *A'* as centers and *G O* as a radius. The points of intersection *C^{iv}* and *C^v* are the two other required centers. The line of the oval coincides with that of the ellipse, as shown by the dotted line, much better in this figure than in the other.

Symmetrical Steps.—Two flights of steps, whether of one, two, or three runs, may be set back to back or face to face, as is shown in Figs. 89, 90, and 91. The middle runs, upon which the others meet, are naturally wider than the others. Figure 89 shows flights of one run. They are face to face at *A*, and back to back at *B*.

When, in symmetrical flights of two runs, the two runs are at right angles with one another, the lower runs may either be between the upper ones, as in Fig. 90 *A*, or the upper runs between the lower ones, as in Fig. 90 *B*. In either case, all the steps rest upon walls, which themselves rest upon the ground. But when the upper run is parallel to the lower one, as in Fig. 90 *C* and *D*, it is better to have the lower run in the middle, as at *C*; otherwise, the upper run is either unsupported, as at *D*, or rests upon walls that encumber the ground below. This is only partially avoided by carrying the run upon arches, as in Fig. 96. When the two flights are parallel to one another they may be either face to face, as at *E*, or back to back, as at *F*.

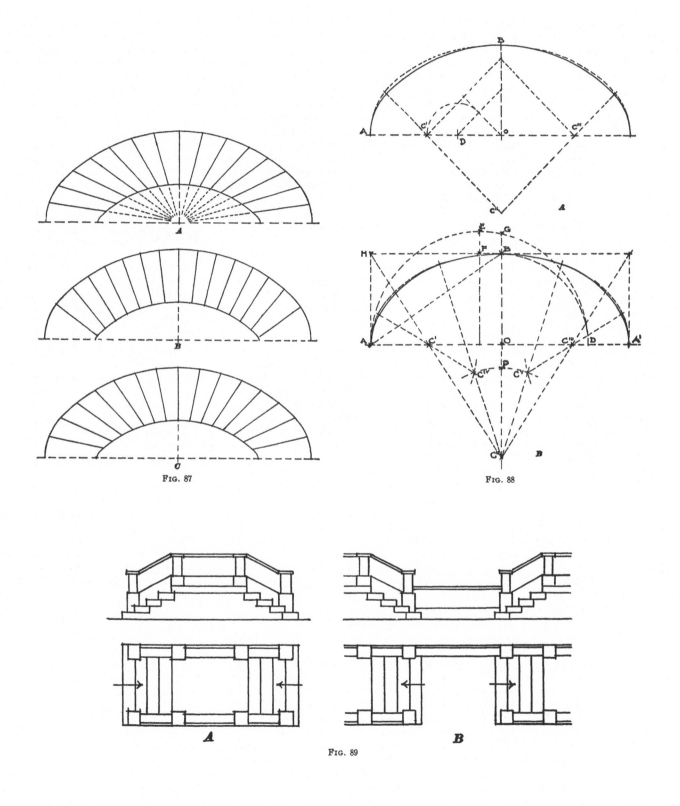

Fig. 87

Fig. 88

Fig. 89

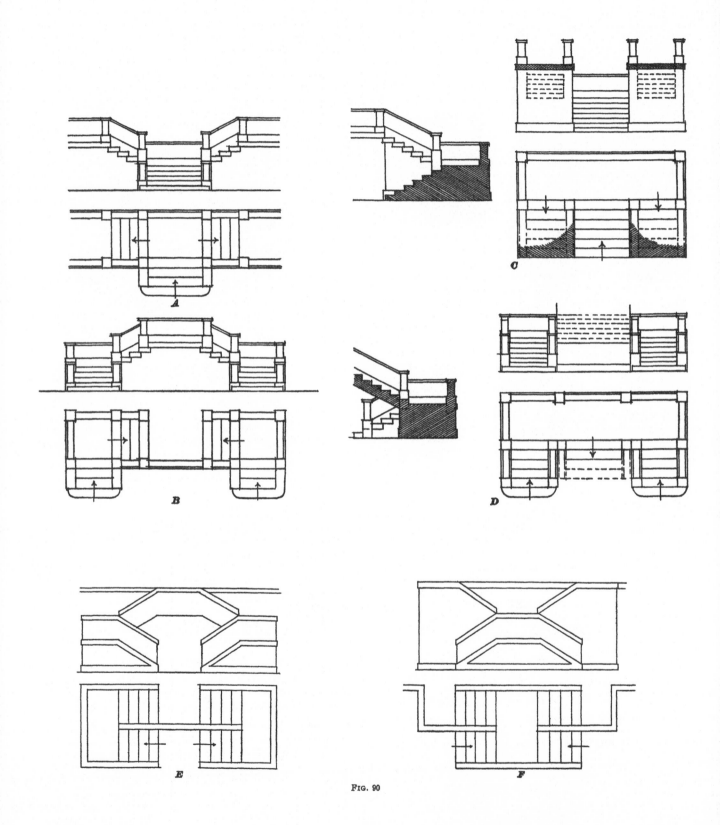

FIG. 90

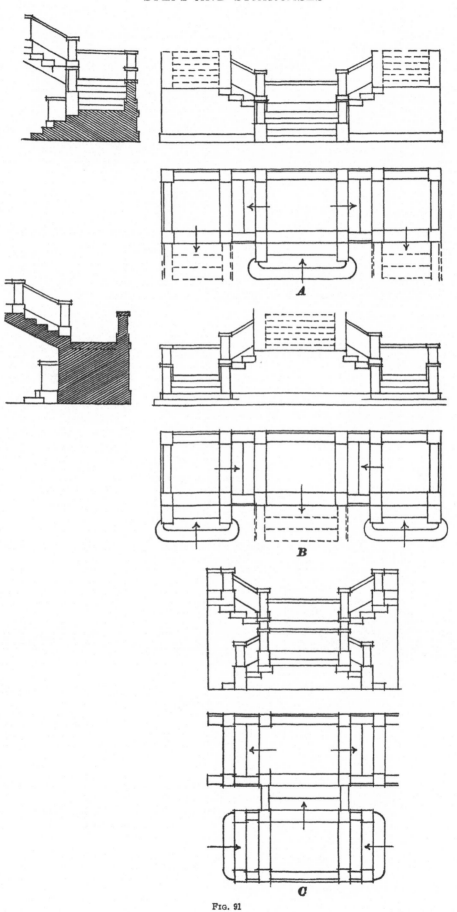

Fig. 91

The same is true of symmetrical steps of three runs, as shown in Fig. 91 *A* and *B*. At *C* the two flights are side by side, having the middle run in common.

But when, in flights of two runs, as in Fig. 92 *A* and *B*, the upper run has the same direction as the lower run, very elegant arrangements result, whether the lower runs are united and set in the middle, or are divided and set on either side. The same may happen with steps of three runs, Fig. 93 *A* and *B*. In either case, a little lawn or garden plot may be laid out on a level with the second landing, as is shown in the right-hand side of the figures.

Cruciform Steps.—Another picturesque and sometimes convenient scheme is that of the Cruciform plan, as shown in Fig. 94 *A*, *B*, *C*, and *D*. At *A*, a single lower run leads to a square landing from which rise three

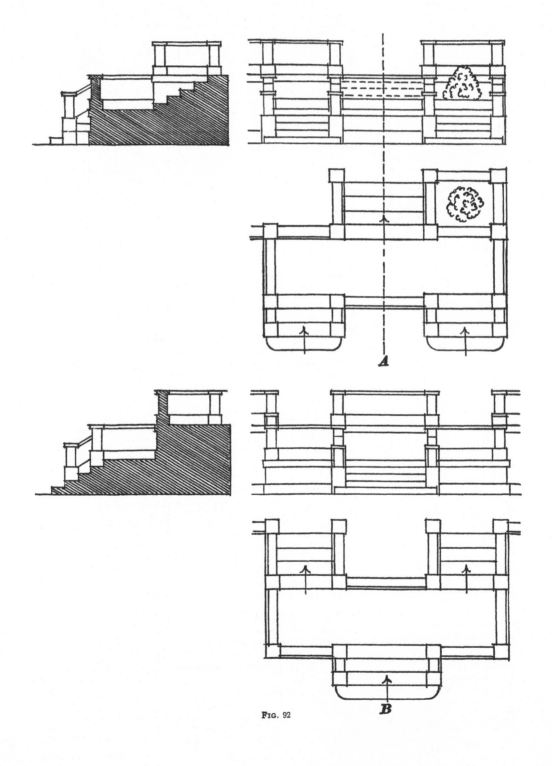

FIG. 92

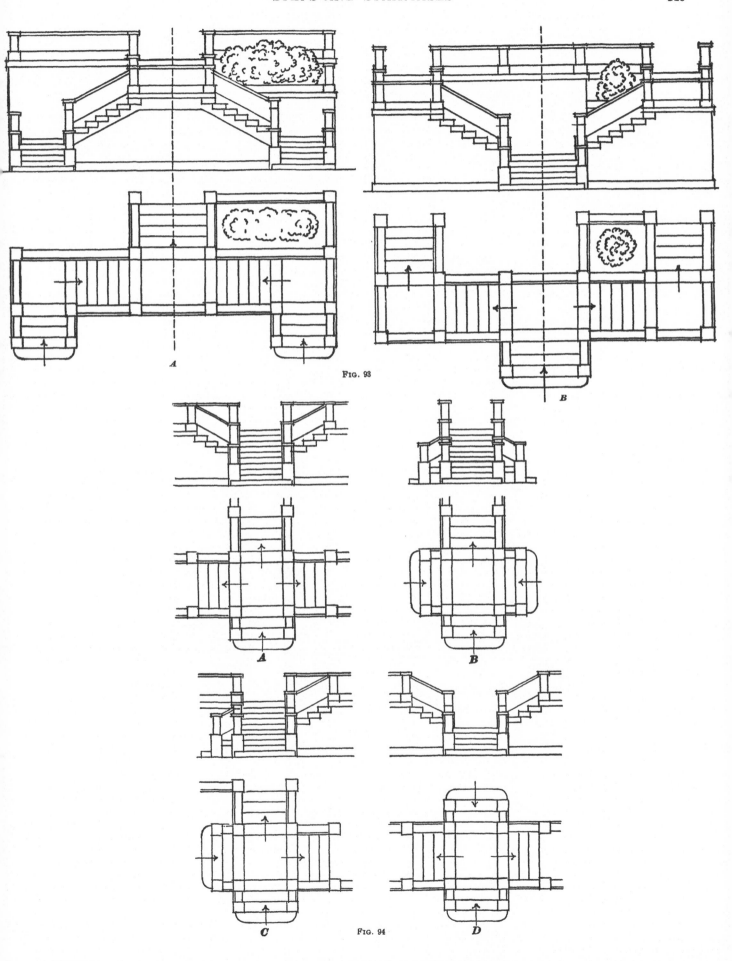

Fig. 93

Fig. 94

upper runs; at *B*, there are three lower runs and one upper one; at *C* and *D*, there are two lower runs and two upper ones, differently disposed. The squares in the corners may in each case be on a level with either the lower, the upper, or the intermediate landing, as may be considered desirable. There is a Cruciform stairway of the fourth type under the dome of the State House at Providence, R. I.

Circular steps of 90 or 180 degrees, or even less (see Fig. 95 *A* and *B*), are often put symmetrically face to face, on account of its being so awkward to put them back to back. In the Museum at Naples is a circular symmetrical staircase (Fig. 95 *C*) which is like Fig. 90 *E*, but built on a curved axis.

Staircases.—Indoors, in the case of a single flight, ascending from one story to the next, the same dispositions are employed as outdoors, the staircase hall being open above, and covered by a ceiling—either flat, vaulted, or domed. If there is a third story, it is better, where it can be done, not to put the second stairway

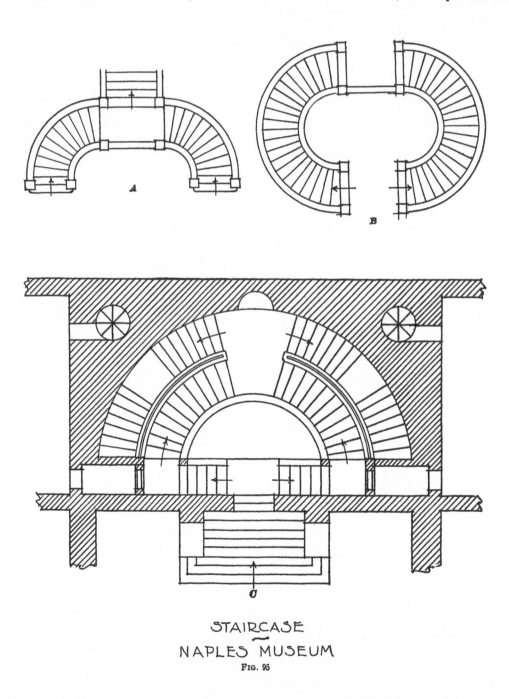

STAIRCASE
NAPLES MUSEUM
Fig. 95

over the first, but elsewhere, nearby, as in the Paris Opera House, Fig. 84. But, as every staircase occupies floor space in two stories, this uses up a great deal of room, and it is more common to put one flight over another. In this case, a symmetrical staircase involves the use of a bridge, either horizontal, as part of the landing, or inclined, forming a run of the upper flight. Both are undesirable, and it is better to build an unsymmetrical staircase, and to attach it to the outer walls at every run (see Fig. 96).

The inner end of the steps, in the lower flight, from the ground floor to the next above, can, as in the figure, always be supported by a wall resting upon the ground, but going no higher than the steps, and supporting the rail, or sloping parapet. The upper flights can then either be supported on columns resting on the posts of the parapet below, with or without arches, or they may rest at one end on the wall, the other end of the steps being unsupported, like a geometrical staircase.

Sometimes there is a wall on both sides, especially when one flight is directly over the one below. In this case, the lower flight is sometimes covered only by the steps of the upper runs, which either rest their ends upon the walls or are supported by intermediate strings.

The lower runs are often covered, and the runs above them supported, by an inclined barrel vault.

Plate XVIII shows three ways in which a staircase of one run may be thus vaulted. As the second story is as high as the first, the rise of the vault is the same as that of the stairs it covers; but as the run of the vault is shorter, by the thickness of the arches at top and bottom, than that of the stairs under it, the line at the spring of the vault is steeper and the wall surface is trapezoidal. Since the third story is not as high as the second, the wall surface is a parallelogram.

The staircases that occupy the least space are those of two runs, side by side, as shown in Fig. 97, *A* and *B*, for the landings are at a minimum. Such staircases are easy to go down, but they are fatiguing to go up, as they afford no breathing places. Moreover, they give access to only one point on each floor, and to reach other points galleries are required, as shown by the dotted lines. But if this floor space is needed for passage, it had better also be used for landings, as shown in Fig. 97 *C*. Such galleries add greatly to the appearance of the interior, especially if supported by columns (Plate XIX).

The place of the parapet, either outdoors or indoors, whether horizontal or inclined, is often taken by some form of fence as in Fig. 98, or by a balustrade, the balusters resting either on the steps or upon the

FIG. 96

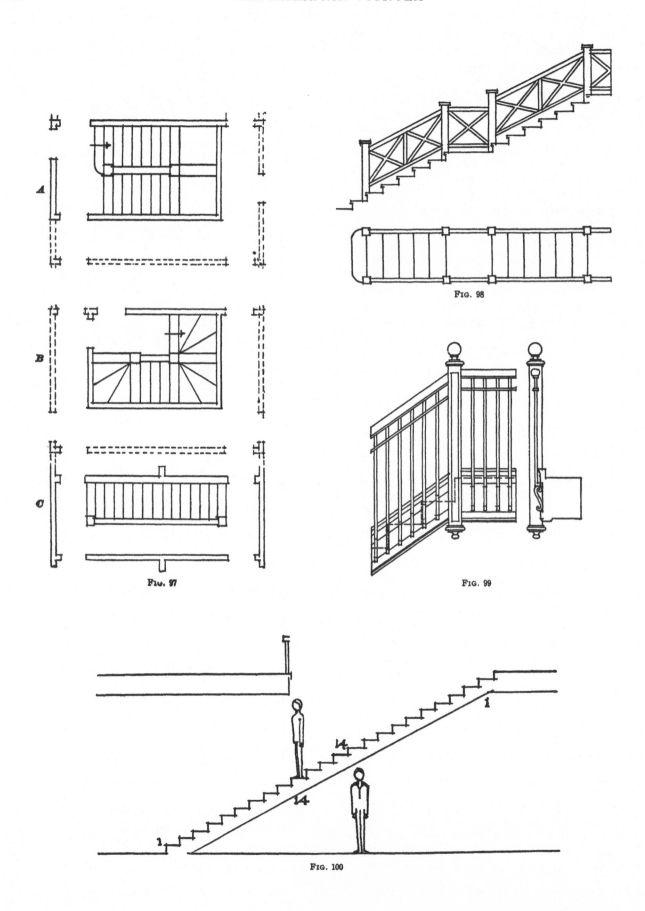

FIG. 97

FIG. 98

FIG. 99

FIG. 100

string, as in Plate XVII. When this fence is made of wood or iron, it is sometimes set entirely outside the string, and is supported either by brackets, as in Fig. 99, or merely by the posts at each end, as in Fig. 98. This virtually widens the stairway.

Headroom.—It is generally possible to pass under a staircase at about the fourteenth step from the bottom, and to pass over one at the fourteenth step from the top (see Fig. 100).

Lighting.—A staircase of one flight, under a high ceiling, vault, or dome, may conveniently be placed in the center of a building and lighted from the top. But if there are several flights, one over another, very little light will penetrate below the upper stories, and it is better to place the staircase against an outer wall. The windows in this wall serve, then, as a sort of vertical lantern, illuminating the whole interior, and do double service, since those on each landing light two stories, and each story is lighted both from above and from below (see Fig. 96).

Circular and Spiral Staircases, consisting entirely of winders, are sometimes built around a circular post or newel (Fig. 101). When built of stone, the riser, or face of each step, lies generally on a radius of the circle, as shown at *A*. But the back of the step is, for strength, made tangent to the newel-post, as at *B*, and the under side is generally cut away so as to give more headroom. Such staircases are generally only a few feet wide. Greater width makes too much difference between the width of the treads at the outer and inner ends of the steps, as is to be seen in the great staircase at Blois.

At the house known as Cooke's Folly, at Clifton, in England, are two spiral staircases one within the other, the inner one for servants (Fig. 102).

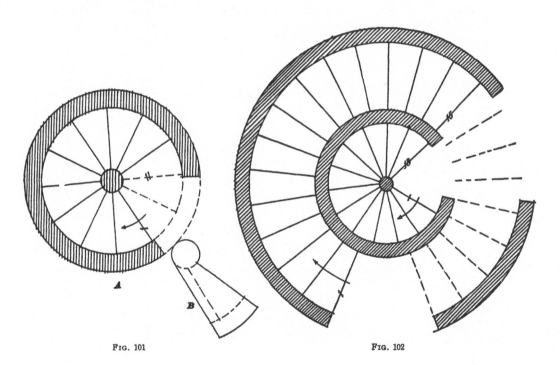

FIG. 101   FIG. 102

Spiral staircases are generally built around a well, which is commonly enclosed with a wall to support the inner ends of the steps.   But there is a circular staircase in the Palace of Caprarola, and elliptical ones in the Vatican and in the Barberini Palace, in which the inner wall is replaced by columns.

At Orvieto is a well, built by San Gallo, 200 feet deep, around which are two spiral staircases of easy grade, one above the other, so that donkeys descend on one side with buckets to be filled, and ascend on the other.   There was formerly a similar double staircase in the Louvre, built by Charles V, and there is one at the Chateau de Chambord, built by Francis I, ascending from the ground floor to the roof of the castle (see Fig. 103).   Rectangular stairways have been built upon the same principle.

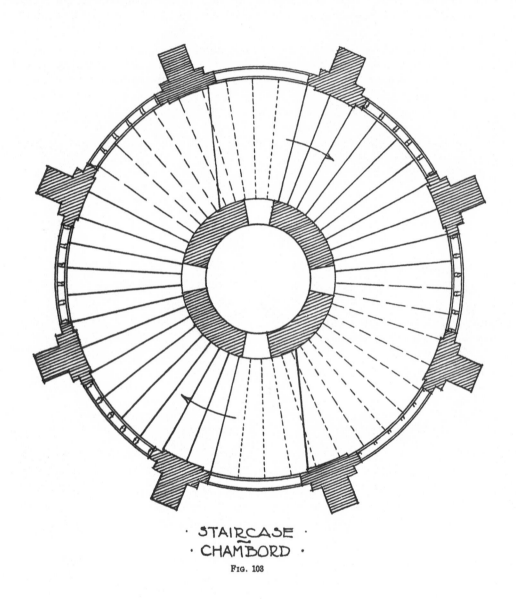

· STAIRCASE ·
· CHAMBORD ·

FIG. 103

PART II
The Plates

A

¼
½
¾
1⅞D
—7¾D—
7D
½
2D   3¾D   5⅛D   ½ 1D ½
5¾D
¾

TUSCAN

B

6 TRIGLYPHS
¼
½
¾
2⅛D
8¾D
8D
½
2D   4¼D   5⅞D   ½ 1D ½
6¼D
¾

DORIC

C

46 DENTILS
¼D
½D
¾D
2¼D
9¾D
9D
½
2D   4½D   6¾D   ½ 1D ½
6½D
¾

IONIC

D

47 DENTILS
13 MODILLIONS
¼
½
¾
2⅓D
10¾D
10D
½
2D   4⅔D   7⅔D   ½ 1D ½
6⅔D
¾

CORINTHIAN

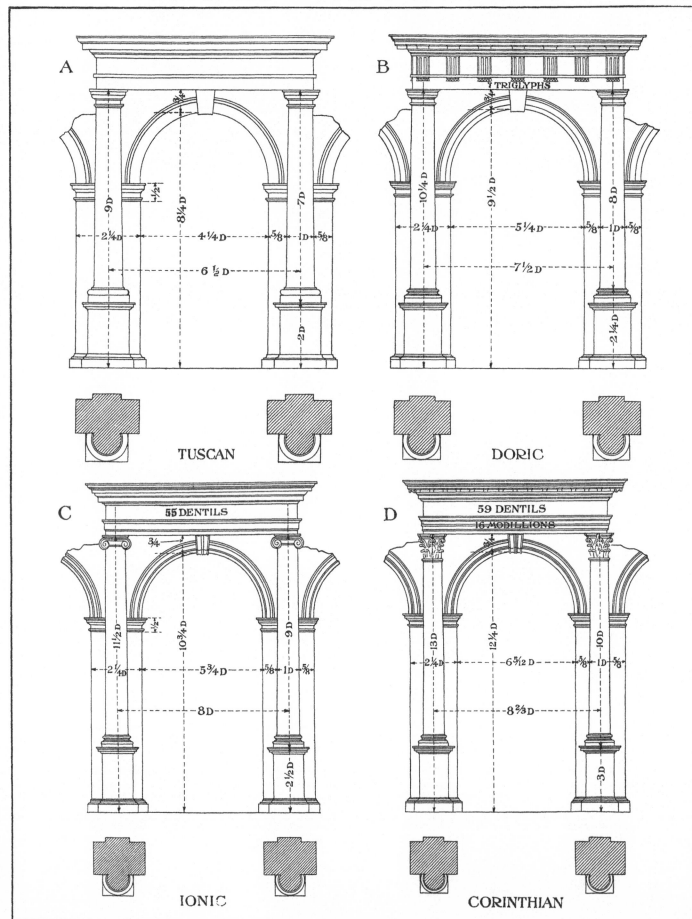

A TUSCAN

B DORIC

C IONIC

D CORINTHIAN

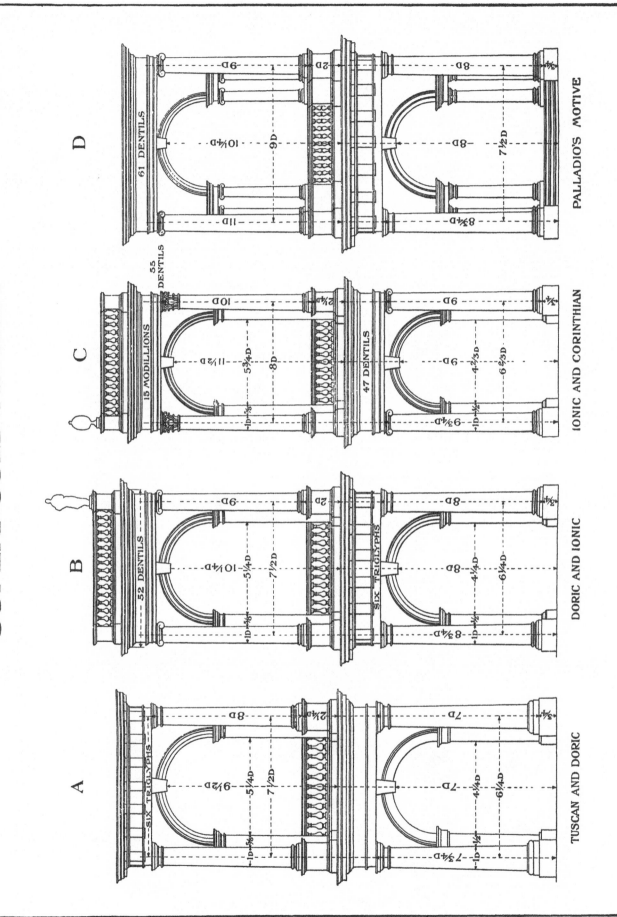

SUPERPOSED ARCHES

PLATE III

A — TUSCAN AND DORIC

B — DORIC AND IONIC

C — IONIC AND CORINTHIAN

D — PALLADIO'S MOTIVE

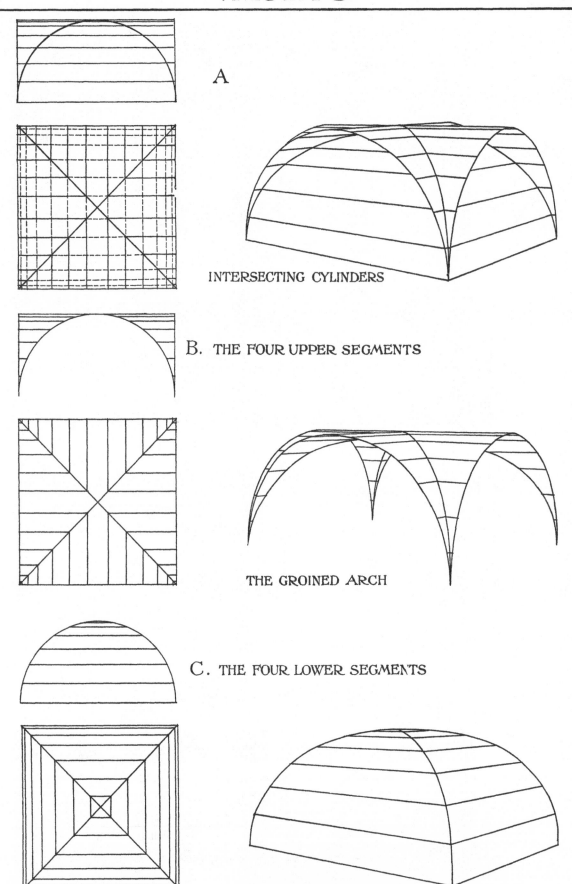

A

INTERSECTING CYLINDERS

B. THE FOUR UPPER SEGMENTS

THE GROINED ARCH

C. THE FOUR LOWER SEGMENTS

THE CLOISTERED ARCH

GROINED ARCHES

PLATE V

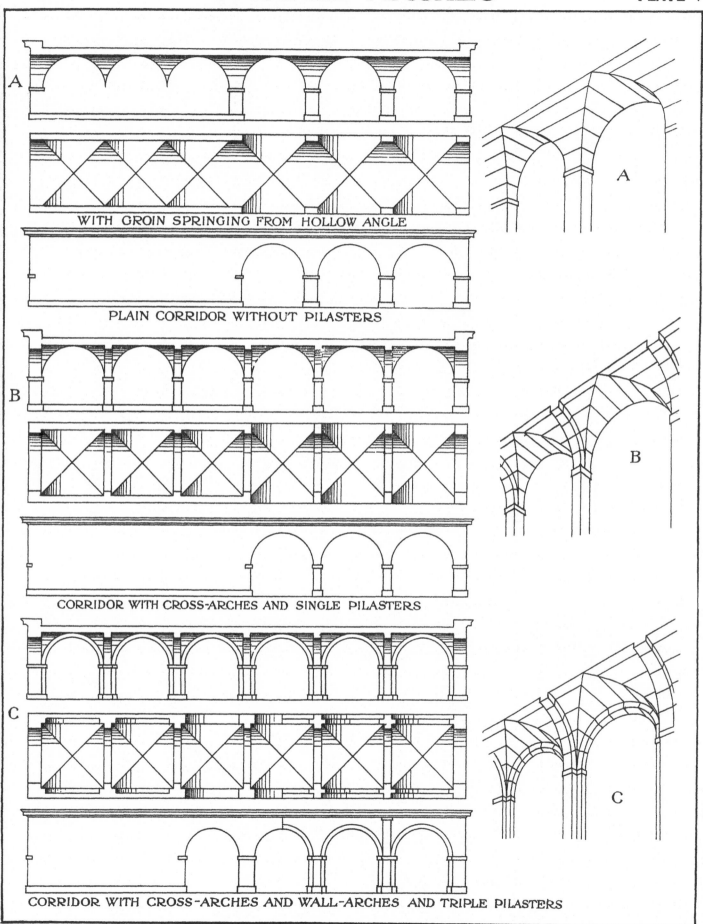

A — WITH GROIN SPRINGING FROM HOLLOW ANGLE

PLAIN CORRIDOR WITHOUT PILASTERS

B — CORRIDOR WITH CROSS-ARCHES AND SINGLE PILASTERS

C — CORRIDOR WITH CROSS-ARCHES AND WALL-ARCHES AND TRIPLE PILASTERS

GROINED ARCHES

PLATE VI

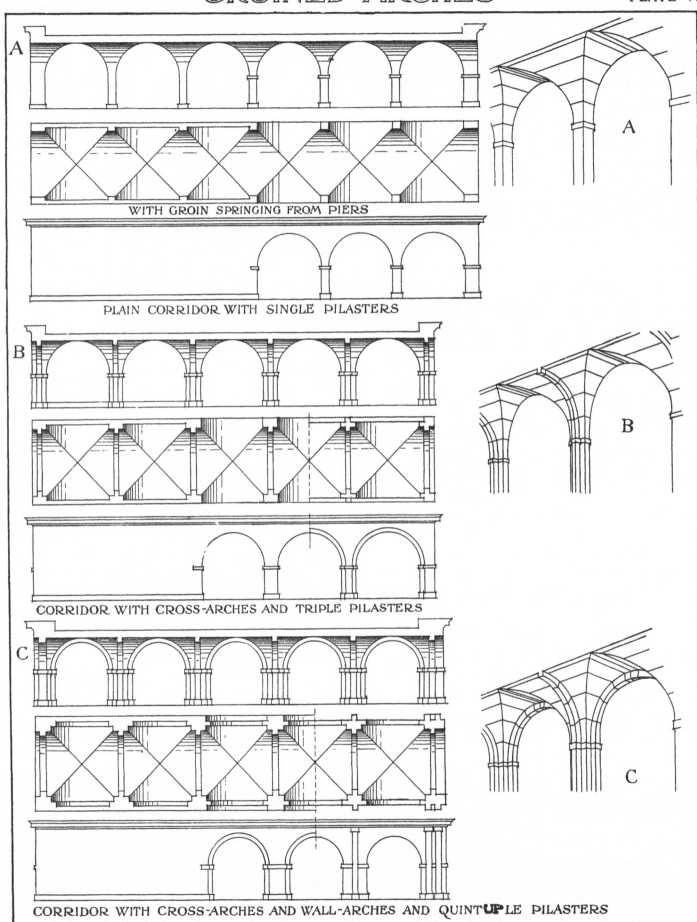

A WITH GROIN SPRINGING FROM PIERS

PLAIN CORRIDOR WITH SINGLE PILASTERS

B CORRIDOR WITH CROSS-ARCHES AND TRIPLE PILASTERS

C CORRIDOR WITH CROSS-ARCHES AND WALL-ARCHES AND QUINTUPLE PILASTERS

RAFFAELLE'S LOGGIA IN THE COURT OF SAN DAMASO IN THE VATICAN PALACE

PENETRATIONS

PLATE VIII

A — INTERSECTING CYLINDER

B, C — CLOISTERED ARCHES WITH PENETRATIONS

E — COVED CEILING

D — FALSE COVED CEILING

GABLED ROOFS

PLATE IX

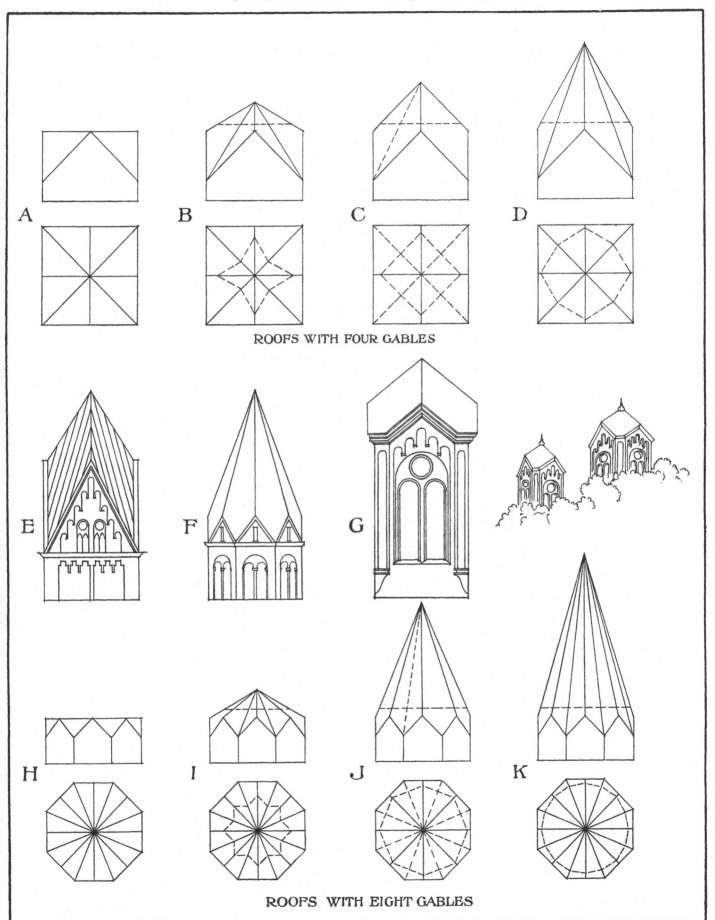

A B C D

ROOFS WITH FOUR GABLES

E F G

H I J K

ROOFS WITH EIGHT GABLES

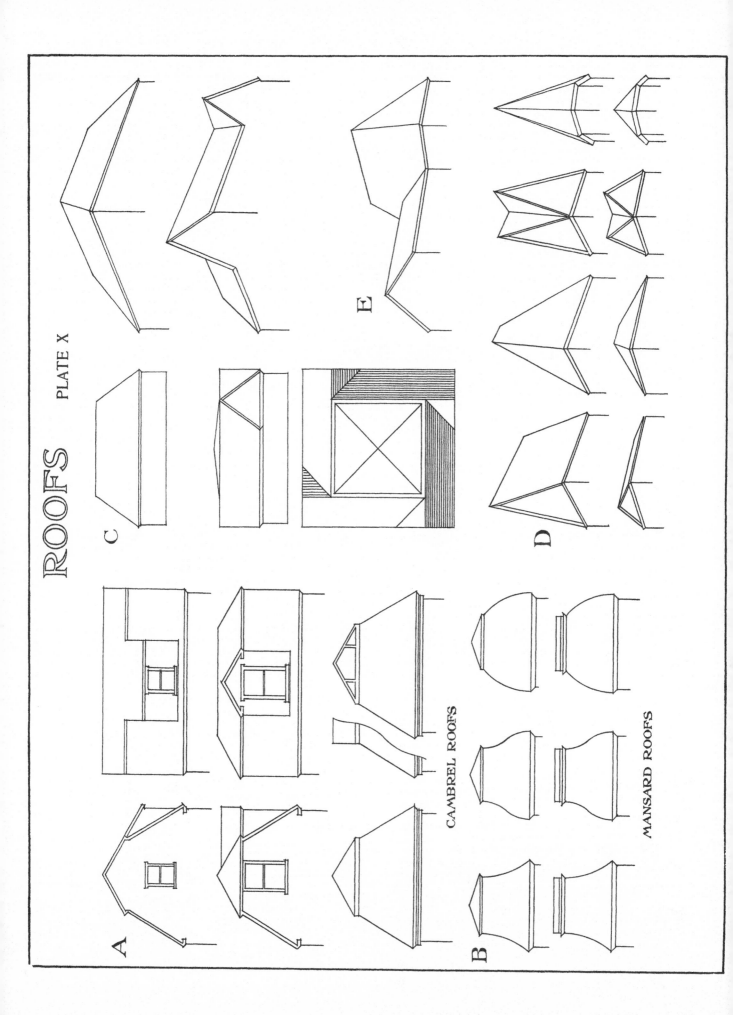

ROOFS   PLATE X

A

B   CAMBREL ROOFS   MANSARD ROOFS

C

D

E

ROOFING IRREGULAR PLANS

PLATE XI

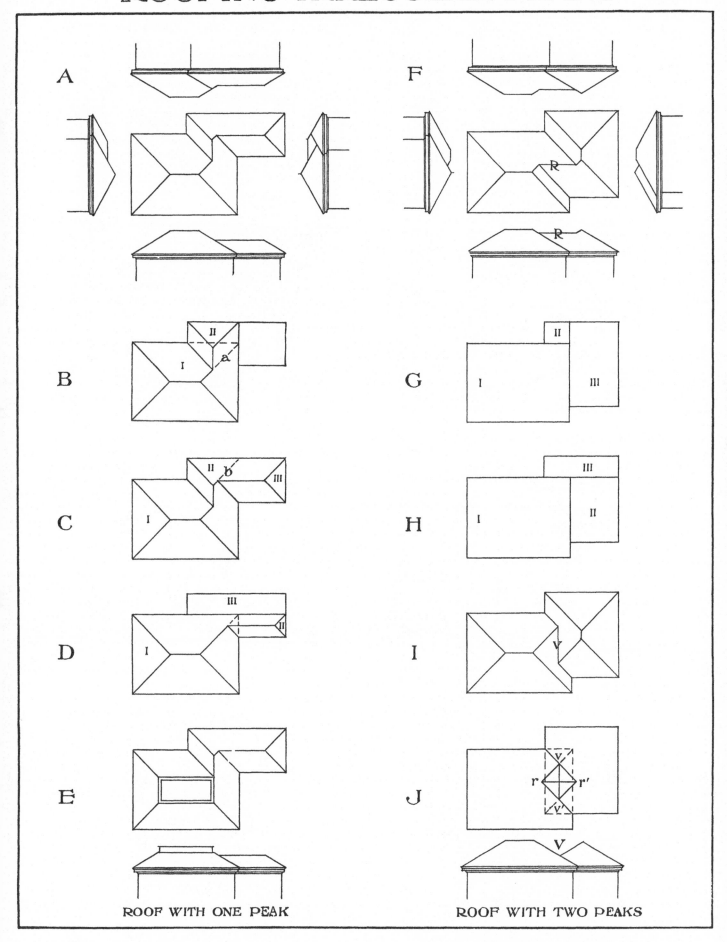

A

B

C

D

E

F

G

H

I

J

ROOF WITH ONE PEAK

ROOF WITH TWO PEAKS

PLATE XII

DOMES

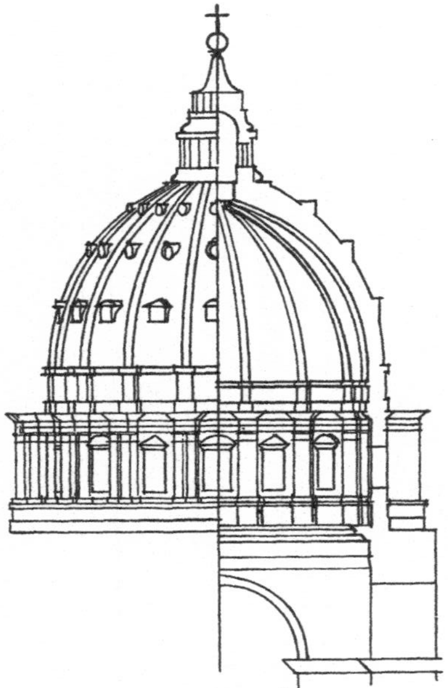

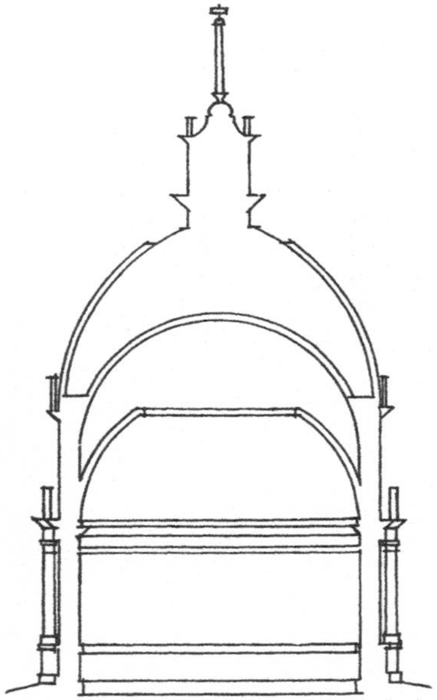

CHAPEL OF THE INVALIDES
PARIS

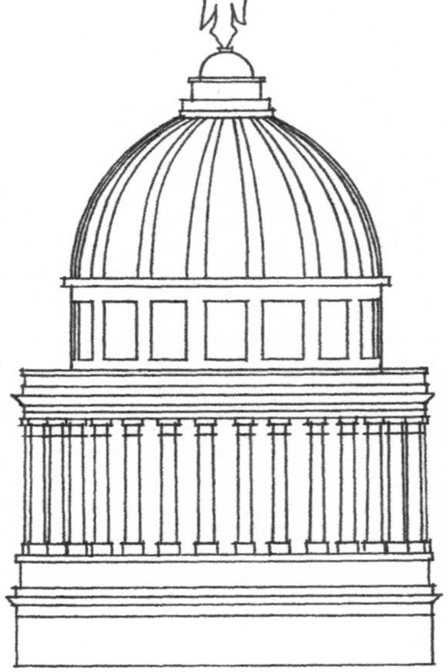

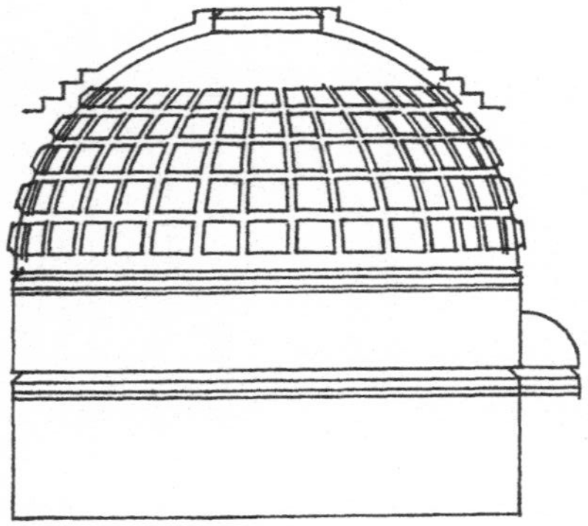

NICHE IN THE VATICAN
MUSEUM
ROME

'THE PANTHEON
PARIS

NICHE IN THE VATICAN GARDENS
ROME

St.PAUL'S
LONDON

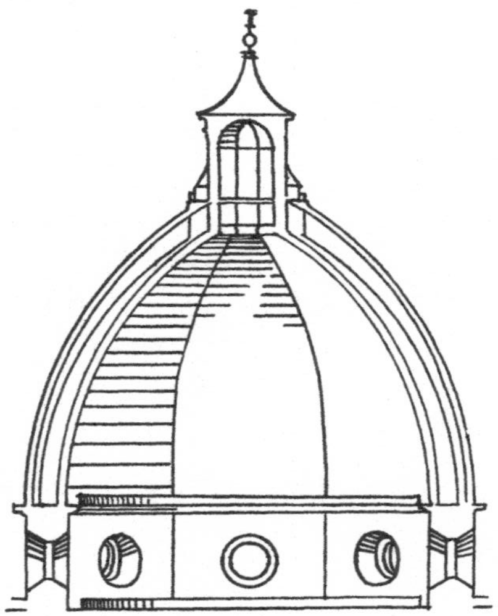

THE CATHEDRAL
FLORENCE

St.PETER'S
ROME

THE PANTHEON
ROME

DOORS AND WINDOWS

PLATE XIII

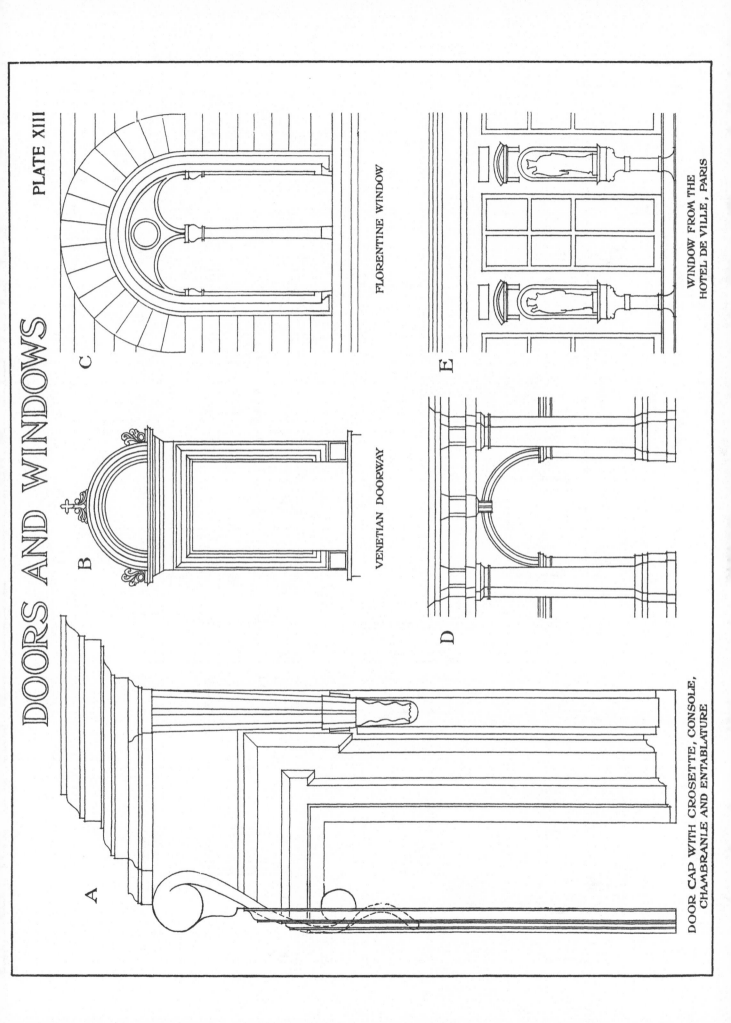

A

DOOR CAP WITH CROSETTE, CONSOLE,
CHAMBRANLE AND ENTABLATURE

B

VENETIAN DOORWAY

C

FLORENTINE WINDOW

D

E

WINDOW FROM THE
HOTEL DE VILLE, PARIS

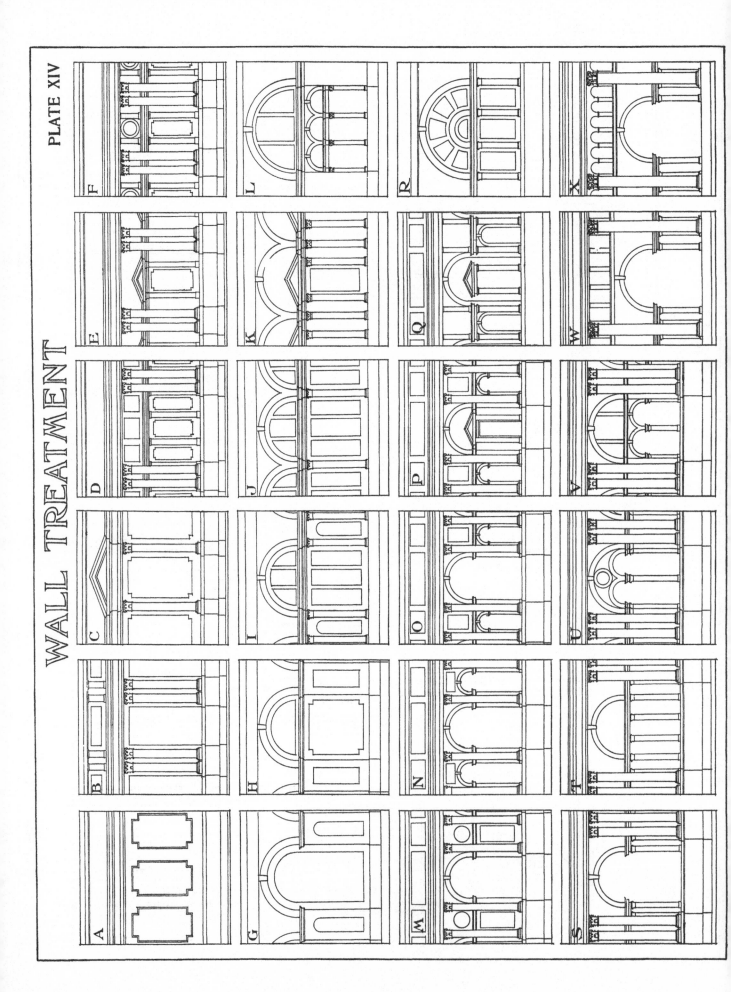

WALL TREATMENT

PLATE XIV

FLAT CEILINGS

PLATE XVI

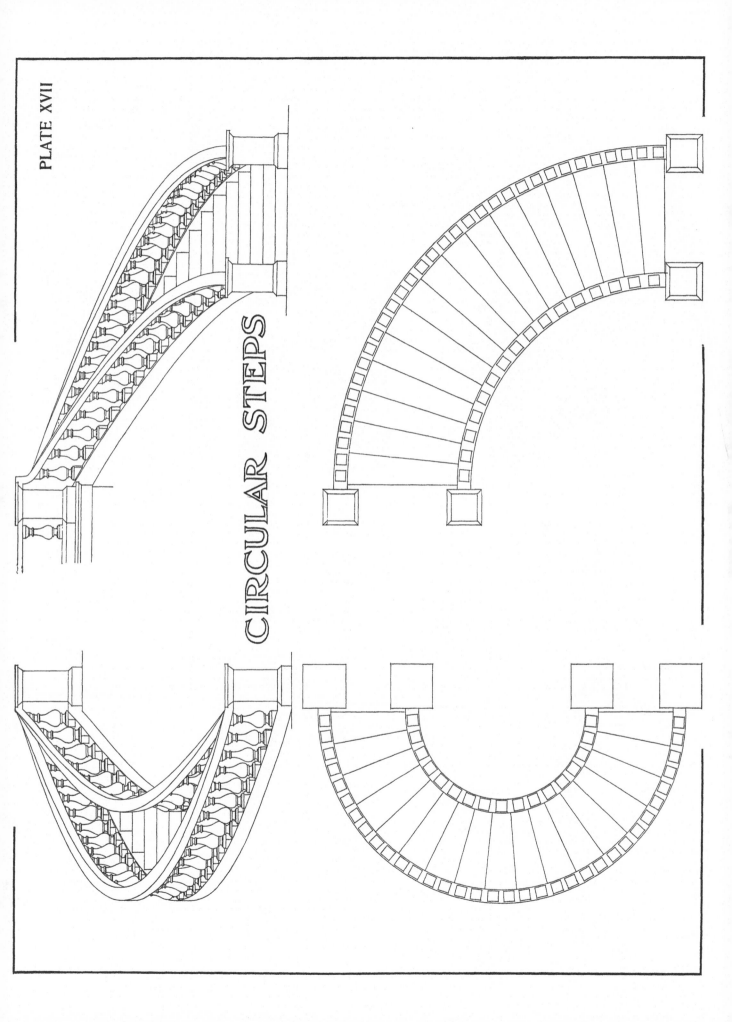

PLATE XVII

CIRCULAR STEPS

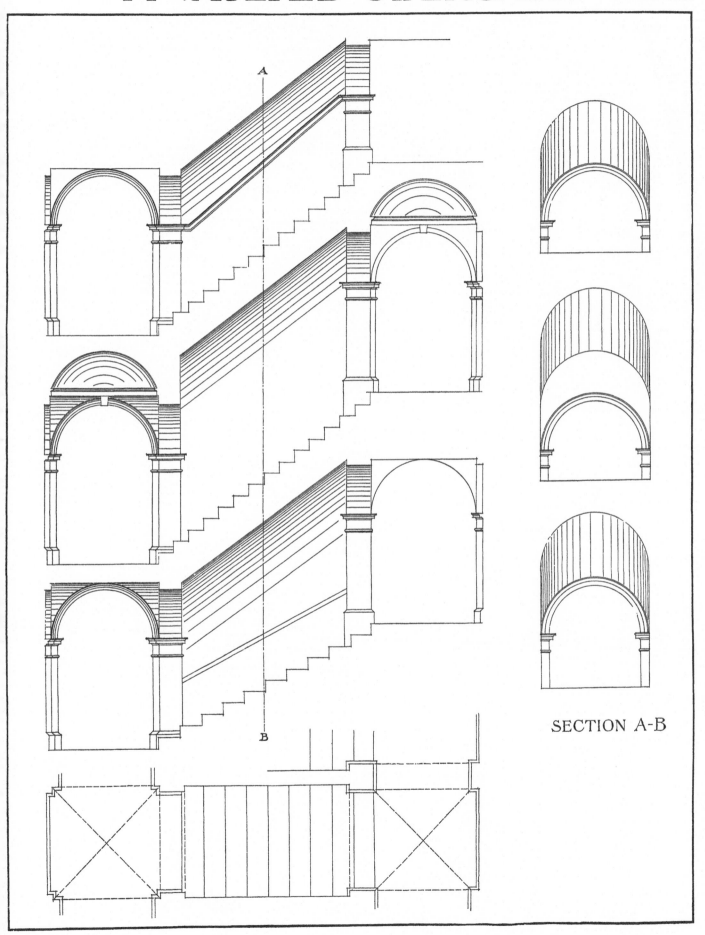

SECTION A-B